Nine Lives—

Nine Case Histories Reflecting the Human Condition

Nine Lives—

Nine Case Histories Reflecting the Human Condition

NEWELL FISCHER, MD

IPBOOKS.net
International Psychoanalytic Books

International Psychoanalytic Books (IPBooks)
New York • http://www.IPBooks.net

International Psychoanalytic Books (IPBooks)
Queens, NY

ISBN: 978-1-949093-44-5

Dedication

To Ruth . . . soul mate

CONTENTS

Introduction • 1

1. Joan—Multiple abortions:
   a compulsion to repeat • 9
   comments • 17

2. Dawn—Black was not beautiful • 19
   comments • 26

3. Claude—Ping-pong? • 29
   comments • 34

4. Henry—Sleepwalking through life • 37
   comments • 45

5. Mary—An unfulfilled life • 49
   comments • 54

6. Sara—"I'm afraid I will kill my infant" • 57
   comments • 64

7. Diana—Self-loathing as a core belief • 69
   comments • 77

8. Frankie—The urge to be beaten-up • 81
    comments • 89

9. Annie—
    Starving to death to keep in control • 91
    comments • 102

Summary and Discussion • 107
Appendix • 121

Nine Lives—

Nine Case Histories Reflecting the Human Condition

INTRODUCTION

have worked as a psychiatrist and psychoanalyst for nearly fifty years, and I have consulted on and treated hundreds of patients. I have never met an alien—someone who was beyond the boundaries of human understanding. Every person is unique, every case offers mysteries and surprises, but the common thread reflecting the human condition has always been visible. Some presentations at first appear extreme or even bizarre, but the underlying conflicts and the haunting demons my patients bring, I know "in my bones," because they reflect shared human conundrums. Unfortunately, for some, these challenges lead to emotional dysfunction, great pain, and suffering.

The well-known American psychiatrist, Harry Stack Sullivan, worked with very ill psychotic patients for many years and emerged from the experience observing, "Man is more human than otherwise." Stated less elegantly and paraphrasing the comic *Pogo*, "We have met them (our patients) and they are us."[N.B. Pogo quote is "We have met the enemy and he is us." from the *Gospel According to Pogo*.] If we look deeply into another person's eyes we see ourselves. Sometimes that which we see leads to a sense of kinship. At other times, the reflection can be frightening, promote interpersonal detachment and self-alienation. Introspection, immersion, sensitivity, and a bit of courage will help the reader recognize himself in the clinical material to be presented. Such recognition may be enlightening.

To shed light on the human condition and to underscore how we all share this condition of being human, I will tell you the stories of nine patients (carefully disguised for confidentiality) whom I have treated in intensive insight-oriented psychotherapy. Their stories are dramatic and valuable. Of course, I can only relate fragments of their narratives, but I will tell you about the most vivid moments and hours I spent with these people, and the times that were most alive and real for me. Though their past histories and surrounding life events helped me understand the moments we shared, such background was once removed from my immediate experience. It was my contact with these nine people that was intense, rewarding, and unforgettable.

Reflecting the human condition, these individuals struggled in life—largely with painful inner conflicts and battles with childhood fantasies and traumata. However, the resolutions they came to did not work for them. They were left with emotional pain and patterns that were self-defeating and compromised their potential for living a fuller life. Understanding their dysfunction tells us much about being human and about ourselves. Comparable to a finely synchronized and oiled machine, when the apparatus is not functioning well, we are more aware of how it works. Cases of pneumonia force us to learn more about infectious processes and the mechanics of breathing. Listening carefully to a child's nightmares can tell us much about his unspeakable worries.

In telling these stories, I also want to reflect and describe through example an important therapeutic approach that puts a premium on the in-depth understanding of the individual's inner world. The treatment was guided by an effort to unearth and understand those forces and structures within the individual that were causing them to hurt or to be caught up in self-defeating and destructive life patterns. The in-depth analytic therapy that I will describe is time-consuming, requires a certain personal sensitivity, and a deep level of immersion. This psycho-analytic approach is based on the conviction that if a person has a greater understanding of himself and the factors that are causing his dysfunction, this self-knowledge will be crucial in stimulating personal growth and in reducing psychic pain.

In the present age of seeking immediate gratification, of fast-food take-out dinners, drive-through religious affiliations, and e-mail courtships, efforts to do in-depth, intensive, and lengthy psychotherapy may be out of fashion. My students, psychiatrists-in-training, tell me that they are required to interview three patients an hour. Therapy is driven by the pressures from insur-ance and reimbursement systems. Medications, primarily tran-quilizers and antidepressants[Closed per Web 11], suppress unwelcomed symptoms, and are often the first and the only treatment modality offered. In such twenty-minute sessions on alternate weeks, the therapist has time to be sure he is looking at the correct clinical chart, check if the medications are causing any untoward side effects, quickly ask how things are going, and then confirm the time of the next scheduled visit. A few patients can be seen for longer sessions and more frequently, but such cases are the exception. Unfortunately this McTherapy also pre-vails in private psychotherapy practices, again driven by eco-nomic forces and social pressures.

These are the two themes in my narrative—(1) an effort to heighten our appreciation of the complexities of the human condition, and (2) an attempt to underscore the importance of therapy that aims to understand the human condition and the deeper dynamics of dysfunction. These themes are inextricably linked.

In intensive insight-oriented psychotherapy, the primary goal is to ameliorate emotional dysfunction and to promote personality growth. In addition, the investigation of the inner world provides a vital avenue to better understand the human condition and better appreciate those inner forces and psychic structures that promote health and the conflictual elements that lead to dysfunction. If the opportunities for pursuing such insight-oriented approaches become greatly diminished by societal pressures, we not only compromise our ability to treat patients in distress, but also we lose an avenue to learn about who we are as thinking, feeling human beings.

To expand on these themes, it is best and most direct to first tell you the stories of some of the people who have come to me for treatment, how I understood their struggles, and how I worked psychotherapeutically to help them.

Before we proceed, a few explanatory notes and a caveat will be useful:

> There are a number of treatment modalities and treatment objectives available to help people in emotional distress. Ideally the specific psychotherapeutic approach chosen is best suited to the unique patient and his struggles. In assessing which approach is most suitable, the therapist brings to the consultation his own bias, belief system, experience, and training.

The therapeutic path I find most useful and effective with many of my patients is an indepth, insight-oriented psychotherapy—a psychoanalytic approach—in which the effort is to uncover and understand deeper levels of the individual's mental functioning. This intense exploration is based on the conviction that if a person has a better understanding of himself and has a greater grasp of the unconscious forces and conflicts that drive his feelings and behaviors, that such self-understanding or insight will lend itself to change and to growth.

A particularly important element of this treatment approach, an element that will be quite visible in the therapeutic work to be described, is called "transference."

Individuals bring to all human relationships their past experience, their conscious and unconscious wishes, expectations, and fantasies. These internal dynamic factors color and mold how one experiences the important people and events around them. This includes how the patient experiences the therapist. For instance, if an individual, because of his childhood experiences—real or imagined—has little trust or faith in the significant people in his early life, there is a high probability he will enter therapy suspicious and expecting to be tricked or taken advantage of by the therapist. In psychoanalytic therapy where the therapist remains relatively anonymous, the shifting of the patient's inner expectations and fantasies onto the therapist is particularly prominent and strongly colors the unfolding relationship. Whereas such transferences may distort the patient's understanding of the external reality of the therapeutic relationship, by the collaborative examining, clarifying, and interpreting these distortions the individual's inner world becomes more visible and understandable. A central focus of analytic work is to allow these transferences to evolve, to be unearthed and to become alive in the analytic setting so that the intra-psychic dynamics can be examined and understood in vivo[no ital in Web, expression in common usage]. In the clinical vignettes described below, the transference elements are prominent parts in the therapeutic unfolding.

Medications and various somatic therapies were not used in the cases included in this book (the exception was Diana). Such interventions in some situations can be very helpful, but in the psychotherapeutic work I was doing, I did not believe this would be useful and indeed might interfere with the "talking treatment" that I felt was necessary.

A caveat is in order: The multiple, interwoven, and interactive elements that contribute to a person's personality and inner world, create enormous complexity and many unknowns in understanding the human psyche. Genetic contributions, a variety of motivational pressures, intra-psychic conflicts, conscious and unconscious imaginations and memories, traumatic events, internalized identifications are but a few of the elements to be considered. Many if not most of these elements are outside of our awareness (unconscious). Whereas the thrust of this narrative is to underscore the commonalities of human beings— "Man is more human that otherwise"—the multiple dynamic variables and this complexity also contribute[agreement] to the uniqueness of each individual.

However, in my effort to coherently tell the stories of these nine people, their personal struggles and their course in treatment, I must by necessity simplify, reduce, condense, and omit many elements of this complexity. Such selectivity lends itself to a distortion in itself in the form of linear formulations, simplistic, and reductionistic thinking. Hopefully this distortion will not obscure the inherent richness and complexity of the people I am trying to describe.

After relating the story of each of these nine patients, I will include a brief commentary to underscore one or two aspects of the narrative that reflect on the foci of this book—elements of the human condition and the importance of insight-oriented psychotherapy.

My intention is to talk in plain, simple, and understandable English. As much as possible I try to avoid professional jargon. I find that when I resort to the use of jargon with patients or colleagues, there is a high probability that I have not thought through the issues sufficiently. Jargon, though helpful as a shorthand way of communicating, often creates more fog than clarity. In this book I also do not cite references from the vast and rich scientific literature related to psychotherapy. Such scholarship, I fear, would lead me away from my primary goal—to focus on the real people whose lives have somehow been compromised and who have come to me for help and selfunderstanding.

I have changed the names and many identifying elements of the patients to preserve confidentiality. I feel confident that these omissions and changes do not distort the main elements of their stories. Though I will be eternally grateful to my patients for telling me about their lives, for the opportunity to help them improve their lives, and for helping me understand more about life, respect for their privacy is essential.

So here we go . . .

1

Joan—

Multiple abortions: a compulsion to repeat

Joan, an attractive thirty-year-old woman, sought consultation because she felt chronically unhappy and she found little in life that interested her. She worked at an executive-level position but was apathetic about her job and was not growing professionally. She was envious and resentful of the people around her who seemed content, and as a result she had few friends. Initially Joan said she did not know why she was unhappy. She described her three-year-old marriage as "loveless" and said that her husband was "bland and aloof." The couple had no children.

In the first several meetings Joan outlined some details of her history and spoke of her unhappiness with her husband. In our fourth session she arrived looking rather nervous, and in a soft hesitant stutter said that she really came to see me because she was a terrible person and did terrible sinful things. She did not know why she was such a "slut." Joan was certain that her depression and chronic guilt were because she had done disgusting sinful things and it was difficult to live with herself.

Joan then went on to describe a pattern starting when she was eighteen years old, of getting picked up by "low-life" men in bars and staying with them until she became pregnant. Soon after she confirmed that she was pregnant, she disposed of the man, and she arranged to be aborted—aborted by a series of "sleazy technicians" in some nondescript houses. Joan had five such abortions in the previous ten years. One of the abortions was performed when she was five or six months pregnant, and she became[past tense] violently ill, almost dying from an infection. The most recent abortion was performed about a year before the consultation and when she was already married.

Joan, in describing this pattern, repeated several times she knew that what she was doing was "crazy," that she was endangering her life, and that what she was doing was "sinful and illegal"; yet she felt herself drawn into this "terrible thing" and did not know why she was doing it. She knew about birth control and prophylactics since adolescence. Joan described the men who impregnated her as "bums" with whom she had little in common and with whom she would never consider having an ongoing relationship. With each abortion there was some initial sense of euphoria—"It was like being cleaned out like a peach with the pit removed and scrapping the insides smooth." Feeling depressed, remorseful, empty followed this euphoria, she tearfully promised herself she would never do it again.

Joan was born two years after her twin brothers. Her development was considered normal and unremarkable. Her father was a physician who had his office in the family home, where her mother served as nurse and secretary. The parents, staunchly religious, preached morality on a daily basis. Prayers were said before every meal, church was attended every Sunday, father was an active leader in the church hierarchy, and many TV shows and magazines were barred from the home because they were not suitable for a "good Christian" family.

Joan always felt excluded by her older twin brothers. The boys played together and ignored or teased her. They seemed to have much more freedom than she did to "horse around." She envied and resented their apparent looseness, and explained, "maybe because they were boys— but it was still unfair." Joan was expected to dress and act properly and to keep clean. Joan vividly recalled a particularly painful form of teasing. At around age four her brothers showed her how they "peed" and kept egging her on to try. They then teased her by saying that she had no "pee-pee—it was cut off." They laughed at the mess she made when she tried to urinate standing up. This was an ongoing theme of the teasing, and she recalled feeling "bad and angry." Joan did not think she could tell her father about the teasing but when she told her mother, her mother reassured her that she did have a "pee-pee[N.B.]" but it was hidden "inside." Joan spent many hours using mirrors and fingers to examine her genital area to find her "pee-pee[N.B.]" inside.

At around age six or seven Joan developed a vaginal discharge associated with itching and burning. She told her mother, and her father lifted her up onto his examining table and examined her genital area. He asked her if she had been touching herself "down there" and used the word "masturbation," which Joan remembered, but it meant nothing to her. Joan recalled that she had been "touching herself" to look for the hidden "pee-pee," and maybe that was sinful and caused the discharge and itching. There then followed a series of examinations by mother's gynecologist and regular douches and suppositories administered by mother. The vaginal discharge persisted into adulthood.

Joan attended an all-girls church-related school and did well academically. She had friends and she was always cited as the example of good behavior. She was permitted to go to parties that were held within the confines of the church programs. If boys were invited to attend, the event was well chaperoned. At age fifteen, a boy who had been invited to the school party kissed her and put his tongue into her mouth. Joan was frightened and thought she might be pregnant. She ran home and reluctantly told her mother. Despite her protests her father insisted on doing a vaginal examination to see if she was still a virgin. Joan felt humiliated and angry. She recalled feeling totally numb from the waist down during his examination.

When Joan was seventeen, she was allowed to go to a school prom that was well chaperoned. However, her date's car ran out of gas, and Joan arrived home two hours after her curfew. Her parents were frightened and angry, and again her father insisted that he do a vaginal exam to be sure she was still a virgin. Joan protested but to no avail.

Upon graduating high school early, Joan was accepted into a prestigious all woman's college. Soon thereafter, at age eighteen, she began traveling to poorer sections of town and meeting men at a local bar. Within a few weeks she was impregnated and then found friends who knew how to arrange an abortion. In the next ten years she had five abortions. When she had intercourse with these men and with her husband, she felt totally numb from her waist down and never experienced an orgasm.

Joan entered analysis; we met four days a week for five years. Many interwoven themes emerged in the material. During the early interviews, when she was primarily relating some historical facts, Joan presented as a depressed, reserved, soft-spoken, and obedient young woman. However, soon after she began lying on the couch and letting her mind and feelings pour forth, she seemed transformed to another person. She became animated, at times enraged and shouting obscenities and then quickly becoming tearful and sobbing. It was as if the smoldering resentment of two decades was unleashed. She cried out, "I hated those filthy men who picked me up at the bar. They smelled bad and they wanted to do filthy things to me and I let them." The only pleasure she had during intercourse was when the man climaxed. At that moment she felt in control and recalls thinking "this poor slob." The men never knew they had impregnated her when they were "discharged." Indeed her husband did not know she was pregnant until she insisted on another abortion. As she raged on about the "filthy men," her thoughts moved to her father. She spoke of his piety, his rigidity, and his bullying manner. At one point she nearly jumped off the couch and screamed, "That fucking hypocrite. What was he doing looking up my cunt?" She then spent the next twenty minutes sobbing and banging her fists on the couch. Amid[prevailing use] the crying and sobbing she whimpered, "and why did my mother let him do that?" This theme of the filthy men and her father came up over and over again, as did her guilt for letting those men, and then her father, "have their way with me." The life endangering abortions were in part her punishing herself for being such a "bad girl". She cried often when she thought of her mother's complicity and asked, "Why didn't she protect me?"

Lying on the couch while I sat behind her and out of her view evoked a series of memories of the early childhood examinations and intrusive procedures. She sobbed and asked, "What were those doctor and my father doing down there?" She could not see them but they were doing "something." Then there were the many douches and suppositories and the further intrusive assaults by her father when she was an adolescent to see if she was still a virgin.

Hesitantly Joan began to express suspicion about me: what I was doing behind her and out of her view. Was I getting excited looking at her body and breasts and hearing her stories? Maybe I was masturbating like those filthy men. Was I listening or doodling? Though Joan became quite agitated by this series of thoughts and suspicions that I was "playing with myself back there," she would not let herself turn around and look. For several weeks, however, Joan insisted on wearing her large bulky coat while she was lying on the couch. She said that keeping her coat on made her feel safer and less exposed. During this time she seemed quite agitated, and I suggested that she might feel more comfortable sitting up so she could keep her eyes on me. Joan quickly responded, "I know there is something crazy about my worries about you, but I just can't get it out of my mind." She elected not to sit up and noted that though she felt vulnerable and scared not seeing me, she also sensed some excitement at the thought that I was looking at her body.

In the third year of the analysis, Joan reported a very vivid dream that she experienced as frightening, but also exciting. In the dream several explorers enter a large cave and are looking for a hidden treasure buried in the walls. Her associations led her back to her childhood fantasies that something was missing—a "pee-pee," but it was hidden "inside." She recalled the many hours spent examining her genitals and then wondering what those gynecologists were looking for or trying to do.

Joan's effort to find the missing treasure (her penis) was reflected in a dramatic incident in the analysis. Joan arrived at my office and complained of having a cold and a sore throat. The session was spent talking about an argument she was having with her husband. Minutes before the session was to end, Joan jumped off the couch and approached me with her mouth wide open. She said, "I know you are a doctor, can you see if my throat is inflamed?"

It became clear as we reviewed this incident over the next few weeks that she indeed was asking me to examine her insides not only to find some hidden treasure but also to repeat the intrusions that were so odious but also quite stimulating. Though she remembered being numb during these examinations, she was also aware of being excited and "turned on." She associated back to the dream wherein explorers were looking for a hidden treasure in a large cave. Joan's thoughts led her to feeling that I was one of the explorers—intruding but also helping her look for something hidden in her vagina. The thought amused and excited her.

Through the clarification and interpretation in the analysis, Joan and I came to understand that her self-destructive and dangerous behavior of getting impregnated and then aborted represented many things at many levels. At one level it was her inner struggle with her family—behaving in a fashion that was totally contrary to her parents' moral and religious standards. The promiscuous sexual activity and five abortions were her expression of defiance of her father's spoken word. At a deeper level she was not only defying him but also enacting his inner forbidden wishes. He felt the need to intrude into her private life and to intrude into her body and examine her to be sure she was a virgin. In one of Joan's outbursts she screamed he was a "hypocrite," sensing that his paternal and medical interest in her body and her sex life had a darker side. She was a quiet, obedient, retiring, and moral little girl who never rebelled against the authority and the rigidity that surrounded her. Even in her adult life she was a model worker, a member of the church choir, and a devoted daughter. Inside she seethed, and in her private life Joan expressed her rage. The life endangering abortions were her way of enacting her self-inflicted punishment and guilt for her sins and her intense anger. When she entered treatment there was a rather dramatic shift from this refined, articulate, controlled young woman to someone who was deeply hurt and exploding with rage, cursing, screaming, sobbing, and suffering with profound sadness. Her loveless marriage provided little help in dealing with the inner demons and conflicts that drove her to self-destructive action and depression.

Another theme that ran through the material and had to be clarified and understood was her lifelong sense of inadequacy. Though on the surface Joan was a very accomplished woman, she always felt deficient and lacking. No matter what her level of success she felt there was always something "missing." In our work it became clear that Joan carried with her a fantasy that her body was inadequate or lacking. She envied her brothers who were freer to do many things that were not available to her, and they also had "pee-pees". Something was missing for her. And then there were those doctors who kept examining her, putting things in and taking them out, and the medicines she was taking "down there." Something clearly was wrong with her body. Everyone was concerned— her father, her mother, and the doctors. This became the nidus for her belief that something was defective about her body, something missing, and somehow inadequate about her. These early experiences and associated childhood fantasies haunted her as an adult and were reflected in her chronic feelings of inadequacy. The multiple pregnancies and abortions also gave expression to this childhood fantasy. When Joan was pregnant she had a hidden treasure inside her— as in her cave dream—but it was a treasure buried by a "filthy" man. She felt relieved when it was extruded but she was then left feeling empty and deficient.

Joan benefitted significantly from the analysis that lasted five years. Her depression and chronic feelings of inadequacy no longer dominated her life. She divorced her husband, commenting, "He was a big mistake," and remarried soon thereafter. She became pregnant and gave birth to a little boy. For several years after the analysis, Joan sent me pictures at Christmastime of her son with a note of thanks.

Joan comments:

Joan's presentation to the world was that of a soft-spoken, refined, even-tempered young woman. She attended church regularly, actively participated in community service, was a devoted daughter and sister and a faithful wife. However, she also sat on a volcano of suppressed and repressed feelings of anger, resentment, envy, and depression. Her inner world that she disguised so well was filled with unresolved conflicts and fantasies of destruction. Her fantasy life erupted regularly in the form of dangerous enactments. In the ten years prior to coming for help she managed to become pregnant five times by "dirty" men and then she arranged to be aborted in ways that were life endangering. After each episode of pregnancy and illegal abortion she felt guilty, debased, dirty, empty, and depressed. She thought of suicide, but believed this would compound her sin.

The flow and form of our analytic encounter resemble aspects of the chaotic life pattern that brought her to treatment. This hesitant, quiet, and refined young woman regularly erupted in my office. It was as if she had waited twenty years to tell someone how angry, humiliated, and empty she felt. She shouted obscenities, vehemently cursed her parents and brothers, threatened to crucify the "dirty men" whom she picked up, and sobbed about her sinful life

Alongside these eruptions in our analytic sessions, Joan was gradually able to see and understand a great deal about her life narrative. As she began to remember and clarify many childhood experiences, the repressive atmosphere at home, the bodily intrusions, her father's need to investigate her body and her own mixed feelings about these hateful and yet stimulating experiences, Joan developed a better understanding of her destructive adult enactments. In particular she could see how by inviting the "dirty men" to impregnate her, she was trying to relive and somehow master the intrusive experiences with her father. Now, however, Joan was the active protagonist and not the passive victim. She then had to destroy the product of this "sinful" activity in a manner that nearly destroyed her.

Joan also came to see how her lifelong feelings of inadequacy were related to the fantasies that her body was defective and deficient. She complained bitterly how inadequate she was, and she envied my wisdom and power. She criticized me for trying to be "too smart and cocky" and on occasion felt "demeaned" if I understood something before she did. "Men have it a lot easier in the professional world," she declared.

Many of these issues were relived and played out in our therapeutic relationship. Her suspicion and agitation that I was gratifying myself by leering at her body and getting "turned on"—perhaps like her father and the gynecologists – became very real and frightening for Joan. The pressured request that I examine her throat was also a vivid attempt to actively repeat the past intrusions. Once Joan could step back and reflect on these intense episodes in our work together, and understand them in the context of reliving past traumata, these moments provided in vivo experiences to better understand and further clarify the unconscious fantasies that were driving her selfdestructive behavior.

In the analysis, Joan and I were explorers—together. We found no hidden treasures in caves but Joan did find considerable self-understanding and self-forgiveness that set the stage for a much fuller life.

2

Dawn—
Black was not beautiful

B lack was not beautiful in Dawn's African American family. In fact, black was to be denied and if possible erased. Black represented African, lower-class, primitive, course, dirty, sexual, and angry—all undesirables and all "black." Dawn a thirty-five year-old Negro[Au/Ed: Use of the word "Negro" OK? Sometimes offensive.] woman grew up in this atmosphere and knew that her "blackness" was to be hidden. She also knew early on that it was not only her skin color that had to be minimized (no sunning on the patio for her) but also her inner "blackness"—her angry thoughts, and her sexual feelings that needed taming. Especially at school or out in public she had to be a very, very good "white" girl.

Dawn came to see me in consultation because she was having panic attacks that seemed related to making public appearances at her work.

She had recently been promoted to a vice presidency of her company and chairing meetings and making public statements was part of her job. In the past, though she often felt anxious on these occasions, in the previous six months she had dreaded public speaking and had acute attacks of panic just prior to four such engagements. Though she was able to appoint a junior staff member to take her place, she knew that her absences were being noticed. Her attacks were associated with intense anxiety and feeling that "my heart would jump out of my chest." Dawn thought that she was "losing her mind" and that during these attacks she would get up and scream obscenities. Between these attacks she worried about having another attack, and she found many excuses to miss work and stay home.

When I first met with Dawn I found her to be a very attractive, articulate, and intelligent woman. She was self-reflective and thoughtful. She reported that though she had generally pushed herself to speak up in social settings and in business meetings, she always had some uneasiness that what she had to say was too simpleminded and that she would make a fool of herself. The recent panic attacks, however, were a major source of worry and they were on her mind constantly.

Dawn was an only child born into an upwardly mobile and ambitious African American family. Her father had started as a stock boy and worked his way up to being the president of the company. Mother occasionally did some substitute teaching but mostly spent her time at home. The couple had a very active social life in keeping with the father's position and aspirations. Dawn reported that she enjoyed a warm relationship to both parents though they always seemed somewhat "aloof and formal." They were very concerned with doing the "right things." Her family lived in an affluent, white, predominantly Jewish community, and they were the only African Americans in the area. Dawn was not aware of any overt discrimination but recalls feeling awkward going to friends' homes and being served lunch by the black maids. Though Dawn and her parents were very fair complexioned, after reading a book in first grade about little Black Sambo, she developed an image of herself as someone with dark black skin like Sambo and having oily kinky hair in "corn rows." Dawn's hair in fact was straight and brown. Though her social life was active and she seemed popular, she often felt that she was different and an outsider in her white peer group.

The parents were involved in many of the community social events, but they also had a group of out-of-town college friends who were also African Americans. Characteristically they were all very fair complexioned, affluent, and had little to do with the "black" community. This group formed their own elite clique in college, and it continued to meet annually after graduation. When Dawn went off to a prestigious IvyLeague college she was warned about not getting involved with those "blackpride people" or those "African" campus groups, and in particular she should be selective whom she dated. She met her future husband in college,and he was also very fair complexioned. When Dawn became pregnant, the couple was very concerned that a "black" gene might have "snuck through" and that their child would be dark skinned.

Dawn and her husband entered the corporate world soon after college and both were successful. They had a child, bought a home in the suburbs, and were comfortable until these "crazy" attacks began.

It is important to note that at the time of the analysis, there was a good deal of racial tension in the United States with many news stories related to riots in urban areas and marches in southern communities. Nothing about these events came into the first year of the analysis. Dawn did not appear to identify with this racial tension and it was never mentioned.

At an early point in our work I wondered to myself about issues that might arise concerning a black woman in analysis with a white man and if this combination might complicate our work or stimulate feelings and fantasies in Dawn or in me. However, there was little evidence to suggest this being an issue for either of us. In fact, I began to see Dawn as "whiter than white" and I was aware of my own negative feelings about her family that was so stridently anti-Negro[Negro OK?]. During the initial evaluation I inquired why she had chosen to see me for treatment rather than consulting with a black therapist. Dawn voiced confusion about my question and went on to indicate there were very few black psychoanalysts in the community, and she would never think of seeing a Negro physician for any reason. She said, "Black physicians were not as competent or as well trained."

As the analytic material began to unfold and deepen, however, Dawn's dreams and association began to make frequent reference to color and color differences. In one of her earliest dreams she went on a trip with a friend and crossed the DC line. She associated this to running off and getting married in Arlington, Virginia. In another dream she was purchasing light pink lipstick, but the saleslady was getting ready to close the shop, so she left without making the purchase. In associating, she said that pink had always been her favorite color in clothing. In a particularly upsetting dream she was chasing some black "hoodlums" who had just damaged her tan-colored car and yelling—"you niggers." In another early dream, a tall dark man was walking on a winter night and the ground was covered with bright white snow, and the glare hurt her eyes. My efforts to explore these references to color differences as it related to our therapeutic relationship did not appear to lead anywhere and seemed "off the mark."

Then Dawn began remembering and talking more about childhood experiences and noted a good deal of early sexual confusion. She recalled spending hours sitting on a rocking chair in the family living room openly masturbating. Mother who was always very proper and rule oriented ignored this behavior. Reportedly this behavior continued for several years. In retrospect, Dawn said with some anger, "This was outrageous . . .

What was she thinking? . . . I was out of control and I needed her to say 'stop'—but she didn't . . . I think this went on even if company arrived. It was crazy, and I feel humiliated when I think about it now." Then in high school she described becoming "a bit promiscuous" and performed oral sex on several of the boys in the senior class. It wasn't particularly pleasant for her but she said she enjoyed and felt "turned on by breaking the rules . . . My parents would have died if they knew." Dawn's sexual life was always disappointing and was something to be "endured." In her marriage she reported that she was always "frigid" and never experienced an orgasm. This was an area that caused a good deal of tension between Dawn and her husband, and he often threatened to go off and have extramarital affairs.

In about the second year of our work, I sensed something was not happening and that somehow Dawn and I were "treading water" in our work. The material and the analysis seemed to be stagnating and not progressing. I was not sure why and I asked a trusted colleague for consultation. This involved my preparing some written summary notes including dream material and a description of the flow in the analysis. I met with my colleague and he listened patiently to my presentation and then asked, "Newell, in your written description of this woman you didn't mention that she is black. How come?" I was a little taken aback and responded, "well she really isn't 'black,' in fact during the summer when I get suntanned we are about the same color." I added, "What does her color have to do with it? I am trying to understand and clarify her inner conflicts, and I'm not particularly interested in her skin color."

My omission in the written summary and my defensive response to my colleague / consultant led me to a good deal of self-reflection. I began to realize that I had been in collusion with Dawn in not talking about her "blackness"—just like her parents had tried to ignore their racial and psychological blackness. Though on the surface I believed that skin color had little to do with the therapeutic process or our relationship, I began to recall my own childhood experiences where black children were very frightening to me. I grew up in a predominantly Negro neighborhood, and I was one of the few white children at school. A vivid memory returned from when I was age seven of being surrounded by a group of angry black girls shouting words I did not understand but they all seemed very "bad." I was knocked to the ground and kicked in the face and sustained a fractured nose. I ran home screaming with blood pouring down my face. I remembered feeling overwhelmed and humiliated. I recalled all the graffiti on the walls near our apartment. There were a lot of "dirty" and forbidden words that were foreign to me but somehow threatening.

As I reflected on these early experiences and memories I came to understand that I did not want to see Dawn's "black" thoughts just as I did not want to see my own "black" and unacceptable prejudice and "bad" thoughts. Dawn had struggled all her life and then in the analysis to be "all white" and to be blind to her inner impulses and fantasies. Recognizing and talking about her "black" thoughts to a "white" man was particularly difficult. Now I was in an unspoken and unrecognized alliance with her to ignore (as did her mother) the darker side of her and of course, the darker side of myself. I could only see this "attractive, articulate, and intelligent" woman, and I was partially "colorblind" to her darker inner world which terrified her and which threatened to explode in her panic attacks.

My self-reflection helped me to clarify my thinking and I was better able to hear, understand, and address some of Dawn's struggle—for indeed, I was having a similar struggle with my own inner "blackness." Our analytic work began to feel more alive and productive. Most of her life Dawn was deathly afraid that her inner world would show through. She fantasized that in the middle of her panic attacks she would scream out obscenities and that she would start to masturbate in public. She imagined the horror on people's faces if she did this—particularly the board members who were all white. This imagery also gave her a sense of pleasure and delight. At a deeper level she really yearned to escape her façade of a nice little white girl. She wondered if her success on the corporate ladder was because she was the "token black." She recalled that every time she was called upon to make a public presentation she felt the urge to scream obscenities. Prior to being promoted to vice president, she recalled sitting at board meetings and feeling the members were being overly solicitous because they saw her as a pathetic little Black Sambo[Is "Samba" intentional for a feminine subject?]. These thoughts made her feel degraded and enraged, and she wanting to scream "fuck you all."

At some point Dawn returned to her thoughts about working with a white therapist— one who was probably Jewish. She had dealt with some Jewish merchants in her community, and she was convinced that they took advantage of blacks, and maybe I would take advantage of her. She said she felt stuck. Jews seemed so competent and well educated, while the black physicians she knew "were like hillbillies."

Dawn spoke at length that she had always felt her life was a "sham" and that her parent's life was a charade. They were all doing "make-believe". She sensed that her façade of being "super white" was fragile and that it could easily collapse. As she moved up the corporate ladder, she felt increasingly fraudulent and angry and that she was more and more vulnerable to being exposed and humiliated.

Dawn and I spent a good deal of time looking at, clarifying and understanding these two images of herself—the little Black Samba and the talented adult women. The origins of the fantasies about little Black Samba in terms of her frightening inner world of rage and uncontrolled sexuality became clear. Her family had colluded with her in ignoring and denying this part of her, and I as her analyst had temporarily fallen into the same pattern.

The panic attacks had disappeared soon after the analysis began and as our work progressed her "passions" became better "integrated" and part of her adult personality. She described a new freedom to stop being a "nice white girl."

She became more outspoken and "honest" at work and could tell fellow board members about things that "really ticked me off." She began to more fully enjoy her sexual life with her husband. One morning she arrived with a broad smile on her face and told me in a semi-teasing manner, "That Black stuff was pretty good last night."

Dawn comments

Dawn struggled with her "blackness"—a blackness that had two primary and overlapping meanings for her.

1. *She was an African American child and woman living and competing in a white community. Her parents reflecting their own self-images, felt that being black meant that you were deficient and repugnant, and they worked hard to deny and erase this racial identity in themselves and their children. It was also true that the white community discriminated and looked down on African Americans— either overtly or subtly. Dawn incorporated and identified with her parents negative view and carried a similar bias and a resulting depreciated self-concept. Her*

identification was confusing to her. She looked into the mirror and saw an attractive tan woman with straight hair—and yet she carried in her head a picture of herself as Little Black Samba. She was uncertain which of the two images her coworkers and white friends saw.

In all aspect of her life—her behavior, her career path, her cosmetics—she tried to be "whiter than white" but she always felt like a pretender—a fraud who would be exposed and humiliated. She also felt like an imposter in her rise in the corporate world. She thought that maybe she was the "token black" and wondered if her fellow board members were over solicitous and thereby condescending. When she was promoted to a vice presidency she felt even more uneasy, fraudulent and more vulnerable to exposure.

2. *In Dawn's conflicted inner world her rage and her sexuality—(her darker side)—were experienced as her "blackness." Her inner world was dangerous, evil and frightening. Her anger and her sexuality were to be ignored, suppressed, and represented dangers ready to erupt. She could not recognize or express her anger—she was always a "perfect" child and a compliant and modest adult. Though control was always emphasized as a child, for years her mother elected not to notice her daughter's public masturbatory activity. Subsequently Dawn provided the controls that her mother avoided, and she became frigid sexually. Dawn was chronically anxious and when she experienced her acute panic attacks her fear was that she would lose control, yell obscenities and masturbate in public.*

It was essential in her treatment to recognize and address these two sources of her anxiety. To focus only on the racial and identity issues—would miss Dawn's deeper conflicts surrounding her inner rage and her sexuality. On other hand, to focus only on the dynamics of her inner world and ignore the hurts and character scars of being black in a white community and with parents who demeaned their racial identity—would miss understanding a significant part of Dawn's ongoing struggle and anxiety.

In this treatment situation, it is also important to underscore the therapist's (my) color blindness. There were two people in the consultation room—both brought with them their past and the dynamics of their inner worlds. The treatment focus was on the patient and the effort was to understand and be therapeutic. However, the therapist was unable to hear parts of what the patient was trying and not trying to say. At times such deafness can result if the message and the pain of the patient is so staunchly defended and obscured that it is very difficult to understand. But also the therapist may not be able to hear because the issues being confronted are too conflictual and too uncomfortable for him.

In my work with Dawn though I raised the issue of race briefly, I did not pursue what the impact might be on a black patient talking freely to a white analyst about being the object of racial discrimination. I too easily rationalized that it should not be an issue in our professional work. It was only after I sensed that the analysis was stagnating, and after I sought consultation and did further self-refection did I appreciate my own blind spot. This freed me up and allowed us to more fully broach her concerns and conflicts about her "blackness" as well as her idealization of my "whiteness."

3

Claude—
Ping-Pong?

C laude was "dropped off" at the psychiatric hospital where I had just started my training. Within an hour after arriving with their son, the parents had to leave to drive home which was several hours away. I barely had time to obtain some historical material from them—and they were gone. I was left to admit and treat their seventeen-year old son who was mute, wearing filthy clothes, and who smelled strongly of urine. From the parents I learned that the mental health professionals who had treated him in their community for several years considered Claude "hopeless," and they had made the diagnosis of chronic schizophrenia [lowercase per Webster]—a label that carried a grave prognosis. The parents somberly indicated that they had three younger children to raise and could no longer devote themselves to Claude.

Since age eleven, Claude had shown a steady downhill course. From a "bright mischievous rascal" he became increasingly withdrawn and distant in his relationship to his parents and peers. He began socializing only with younger children. His grades grew progressively worse. The only bright spot that father could recall in this deterioration over the previous six years, was in the eighth grade, though Claude had all *D*'s on his report card, he worked hard at spelling and became a finalist in a county-wide spelling bee. This was the only activity in which Claude seemed to show some interest and enthusiasm. However, this too was short lived. As time passed, Claude became more and more remote, and his school record deteriorated. During the eight months prior to this hospital admission, he spent much of his time at home sitting slumped over a living room chair and frequently he did not respond to, nor appear to recognize friends and family members. Claude was virtually mute. He ate poorly and neglected his personal hygiene. He had seen a series of mental health professionals in his community for several years and he seemed to be getting worse. The family was told they should try to bring him to the private hospital where I was working but they cautioned the family that their son would probably end up in a longterm residential state facility. When the parents told Claude about the arrangements they had made to hospitalize him, he became totally rigid and noncommunicative. Father had to dress, wash, and carry Claude to the station wagon, where he remained rigid and mute for the several hour ride. He refused to eat and he soiled himself.

My first contact with Claude was when I went to his room to greet him. He was a tall lad and was quite thin and underweight. His hair and clothing were in disarray and looked and smelled as if he had not bathed in several weeks. He reeked from urine. He stood in the corner of his room with his head down and his arms dangling. Occasionally he looked up suspiciously. He would not sit down and would not respond to any of my questions. For the next two weeks Claude said virtually nothing. I came to his room to see him six days a week. Often when I arrived at the hospital unit I found him slumped over a couch in the community lounge area; at my prodding he would grudgingly get up from the couch and very slowly follow me back to his room where he remained standing with his head bowed down and only rarely mumbled.

My initial efforts to develop some sort of relationship with Claude I suspect were stiff, stereotyped, and naive[naïve first spelling in Webster]. First I was warm, friendly, and tried to be helpful. He did not respond. I sat and watched TV with him in the lounge, but he seemed unaware of my presence. I then tried the silent "waiting game"; he won that hands down. I then made what I thought were perceptive, insightful, and interpretive comments about the meaning of his silence, anger, and negativism; he seemed unimpressed with my scholarship.

I arranged for a psychopharmacology consultation thinking that some medications might be helpful, but Claude refused any medication, and I was not willing to try to force or try to "trick" him into complying.

We remained in this stalemated situation for about two months—Claude virtually mute, head bowed, and I trying to find some way to engage him and feeling increasingly frustrated.

Then one day after spending fifteen minutes going through our ritual of him standing in the corner and me sitting on the soft chair, I stood up and blurted out, "Come on, Claude, let's play ping-pong." To my surprise he slowly and grudgingly followed me out to the lounge play area. With my urging he picked up the paddle and started to play, but seemed totally uninterested and uninvolved. If the ball was out of his reach, he did not try to hit it. He watched the ball bounce and pass. Initially I tried to "underplay" him—that is, as we volleyed I thought maybe I could let him beat me. This was impossible. Unless I merely dropped the paddle to the floor he could easily beat me at playing poorly. I then thought maybe it was unrealistic and indeed condescending to even try to miss hit the ball.

I could not do it. So I began to play for "real" and other than a few shots where I missed the table, I won all the points. I realized, particularly after I slammed a few volleys, that I was enjoying "beating" him, and indeed I was quite angry with him. For the past two months it felt as if he was mocking me and making me feel impotent and useless. The nursing staff on the unit was beginning to wonder about my "foolishness" in trying to work with this hopeless boy. As we played on I realized I really wanted "to beat the crap out of him". Claude did not seem to care and for the next week we continued in this fashion, and though he was involved enough to hold the paddle, it seemed to mean little if he hit the ball or if he just watched it bounce. Nevertheless, I continued to play with considerable vigor. One day at the end of a very long week, feeling tired, and despairing of the progress of our "tournament," I remained in his room and did not ask him if he wanted to play ping-pong. Toward[prevailing use] the end of a nearly silent hour he looked up at me and said the longest sentence I had heard from him since his admission to the hospital. In an impatient tone he asked, "Well, do you want to play?" In an effort to disguise my astonishment, I nonchalantly replied, "OK."

Claude's game began to improve. Every afternoon he and I played a series of three games. He still rarely spoke and only occasionally looked directly at me, but our contest was now obviously an involving one. He played hard, and he improved dramatically. In the beginning, I generally won the three-game series, but I had to work at winning, and my game improved considerably. One day during a heated series, Claude hit a hard forehand slam and in my efforts to return it, I tripped over my feet and fell to the floor. As I gathered myself up, I noticed that Claude was broadly smiling. This was the first affective response I had seen from him since me met. We continued to play. I was not sure what was going on in Claude's head but clearly there was some shift in our engagement. He enjoyed knocking me down.

For the next month Claude and I played ping-pong daily. He developed a rather fierce and accurate slam that clearly pleased him. I managed to keep a slight winning edge, but only with much strenuous effort and concentration. This drama that we acted out every afternoon, and the meaningful and growthful encounter it seemed to suggest, was carried over to other spheres. Claude began to relate to other patients, first by challenging and thrashing them in ping-pong and then by slowly become engaged in other activities with them. He became much more careful about his attire and personal hygiene. He became involved in occupational therapy sessions and became the floor champion Scrabble player. Before our daily three-game series, Claude and I would volley for about ten minutes, and it was during this time that we had our most intimate verbal exchanges. He told me a bit about his home and revealed a deep resentment toward his younger siblings who he felt were much smarter than him. He felt his parents had given up on him, and he said he didn't care. If I pushed him too hard for details about his grievance and his life, he began to volley in a limp apathetic way. This was a sure sign that I had become too intrusive. After our games we routinely had a Coke[trademark] together, and he always insisted on treating. Once he asked my advice about a pair of earrings he was making for a student nurse he liked from afar. He shyly confided to me that he had let her beat him in ping-pong.

After Claude had been in the hospital for eight months, it was thought advisable for him to enter a residential school in another state that was closer to his home and family. It was planned that he would continue therapy at the school and that his family would have the opportunity to be with him to become more involved in his treatment. He could also complete his high school education. Claude and I spoke about this for many hours—usually as we volleyed or had Cokes. He was reluctant and frightened but willing to give it a try. As his discharge day approached he grew increasingly apprehensive but his profound regressive behavior did not reappear. As we said good-bye on his last day, Claude had tears in his eyes. I also felt sad. I was impressed with the strength and firmness of his handshake.

Claude comments

It was unfortunate that I had to treat Claude in a vacuum, that is, I knew very little about his life and his development prior to him arriving at the hospital, and he disappeared from my view soon after he was discharged. Claude's parents were worn-out and felt hopeless about their son. He had been visibly ill, withdrawn and noncommunicative for nearly six years, and their efforts to help him seemed to go nowhere. The local mental health professionals had also given up hope. Claude's parents had three younger children to raise and they worried about how Claude's illness was affecting his siblings. Claude was deposited at the hospital and in the eight months that he was there his family rarely visited. Upon discharge from the hospital I met with Claude's father briefly, but he indicated that it was a long drive home and he was anxious to leave. Claude then disappeared from my sight. My many follow-up phone calls and letters to Claude and his family were not answered.

As I met with Claude hour after hour, six days a week for several months, trying to make some meaningful contact with him, I began to get a sense of his isolation and the despair hiding behind his protective withdrawal, for I too was beginning to feel increasingly alone and despairing. He seemed to be ignoring me, or at best tolerating me. Trying to engage this seventeen-year-old "scarecrow" in a darkened room that reeked from urine was becoming intolerable and seemed hopeless. I knew I had to do something to break this painful deadlock. My impulsive challenge to play ping-pong and then my pleasure in slamming the ball at him reflected my growing frustration and my mounting anger. In our combative "play," I had translated his personal struggle with his inner demons as a struggle between the two of us. He wanted to "blow me off," and I insisted on "slugging it out" with him. This was liberating for me and ultimately helpful for Claude.

Initially Claude just stood at the end of the ping-pong table and limply held the paddle. I could not "underplay" him. He was an expert at losing. It also felt "crazy" and dishonest to try to miss-hit the ball. I could not do it. Then my increasing vigor and blatant aggression seemed to interest him, and he wondered why one day I didn't invite him to play. And so our tournament began.

Our play became increasingly animated and competitive. Our relationship shifted from frustrated-angry-therapist versus passive-non-communicative patient into two competing combatants—we both wanted to win. In these new roles we were both fully engaged, and our relationship was changing and seemed to be growing. If I tried to revert to being "therapeutic", that is, if I asked too many questions or tried to make clarifying comments—, he let me know by becoming limp in our play and I knew I should "back off."

We both worked hard at winning. Our struggle was serious, and yet in our battle no one got killed or even hurt. At the end of our daily match we put down our weapons and went and had a Coke together. He was in charge—he wanted to pay and that was fine with me. I learned to respect his direction. The growth in our relationship spread and he started relating, hesitantly to be sure, to other patients and staff. His skills at spelling, a high point in eighth grade, again blossomed, and he was an excellent Scrabble player.

Over the years I've wondered what happened that opened a path for Claude to emerge, from his isolated and regressed state—at least for the last three months of his hospital stay. I suspect Claude's improvement was not because he developed some new self-understanding. Though I think it was helpful that in our work together we tried to attach words to his inner struggles and to his inner demons, our engagement was far more visceral and nonverbal. When our relationship was floundering on despair and hopelessness, we both sensed it and we shared an urgency to save some thread of engagement. In our ping-pong bout we were both struggling to establish some kind of relationship - some way to communicate. It had to be genuine and "for real"—no pretense. I appreciated his silent desperation and his protective withdrawal, for I too was feeling desperate and alone in the treatment. He sensed that like his parents I was getting worn-out and perhaps ready to withdraw. Together we found something to keep us engaged and afloat. The relationship evolved and was growthful—for both of us.

In the large and rich literature on the nature of therapeutic action (i.e., what happens in therapy to make it therapeutic) one of the principle areas of debate is if it is the insight and understanding that is therapeutic or is it the relationship or interaction between patient and therapist that produces change. Though I will address this issue at some length in the closing discussion of this book, in the work with Claude, it seemed clear that something in our relationship became engaging and helpful. From behind his protective wall a picture emerged of the child the parents remembered from a dozen years earlier—a "bright and mischievous rascal." The child had not died nor had he been obliterated. Rather, he had gone into hiding.

It was unfortunate that I was unable to see if the value of this brief engagement was sustained in the years following Claude's hospital stay. I remained hopeful.

4

Henry—
Sleepwalking through life

Henry felt as if he were "sleepwalking" through life. He sensed that he did not fully experience the world around him. When people told him about exciting and interesting happenings — books, movies, life events—happenings they had shared—he felt he "didn't get it." He often asked himself, "Why were these people so happy or involved?" He felt bewildered and that he was only half awake or somehow "out of it and in a fog." He sought treatment because he sensed, "Something is wrong with me." He complained, "I'm missing life. I feel like I'm half dead."

Henry was an only child born unexpectedly to parent in their midforties. He described his mother as emotionally labile, and prone to outbursts of anger and childlike tantrums. Small upsets seemed to overwhelm her, and Henry recalled feeling terrified by these episodes. Father was seen as a strong, logical, stoical, and a steady person, but he spent a great deal of time away at work. Henry greatly admired his father though he had very few memories of him. When his father was at home, he remained distant and often silent. Henry yearned to be closer to his father and to grow up strong like him though when he tried to describe his father, he could remember very few details. He said that he especially missed his father when he was away on business trips. At those times his mother was even more unable to cope with life and more out of control and frightening.

When Henry was eight years old, and after much coaxing from Henry and his mother, his father agreed to take him on a fishing trip. This was their first such adventure together. Because Henry and his father had to leave very early in the morning, it was arranged that Henry and his father would sleep in the large bed in the parents' room and mother planned to sleep in Henry's room.

Sometime during the night his father suffered a massive heart attack. Henry's mother heard noise from the bedroom and discovered her husband on the floor. She called the police, the fire department, neighbors, and the emergency squad. There were shouting, sirens, flashing lights, and attempts at CPR on the bedroom floor, before father was removed in a screeching ambulance. Henry's father was pronounced dead at the hospital. Henry reported that he slept through the entire episode and woke the next morning feeling disappointed that the fishing trip was not to be.

After his father's death there was a funeral and a period of mourning when a few relatives arrived, but Henry had hardly any memories of these events except that his mother seemed very sad. He returned to school, and he noticed that classmates seemed to avoid him and that made him feel more lonely.

Henry described his life growing up as uneventful and "muted." He was shy and uncomfortable at school. He had a few friends, but could not recall much of what they did together. He did not remember any of his teachers' names and none whom he particularly liked or disliked. In a sad tone he reported, "I just sort of rolled along—no ups and no downs."

He had a girlfriend in high school, but that lasted only a few months, and he commented, "that didn't work out—she wasn't interested." His mother took a job as a secretary and worked long hours, and Henry spent a great deal of time alone. He attended a local college and did well scholastically but participated in few activities outside of school, and he had a limited social life. He obtained a degree in accounting and then worked at a large accounting firm that he described as "not very interesting." Henry shared an apartment with a fellow worker, and they went to the movies often. His mother was diagnosed as having ovarian cancer, and she died within six months of the discovery of her tumor. Henry felt sad, but this too was "muted," and he thought he should have felt more.

Henry came to see me just prior to his thirtieth birthday and stated, "I feel like I am sleepwalking through life and like I am half dead. Something is wrong with me He was a nice looking young man but clearly restricted and contained. Though he described feeling depressed, he showed little emotion. He was soft-spoken and had difficulty maintaining eye contact. Henry made it clear he was unhappy with his life and wanted help.

Henry and I agreed to meet five times a week in psychoanalysis. In the second year of our work together an unusual pattern evolved. Henry, who was always on time and never missed an appointment, arrived, lay down on the couch, and began to talk about his work. After about ten minutes he promptly fell asleep. This pattern began to happen regularly and he slept during three of his five sessions a week. If undisturbed by me, Henry would sleep the entire session. His sleep appeared deep, and he reported it was dreamless. He felt embarrassed, bewildered, and then angry with himself for wasting so much time and money. On several occasions he drove to my office, parked in the lot, and if he was a few minutes early, he sat in his car listening to the radio.

On these occasions he fell asleep and woke up in an hour and then drove to work. This pattern lasted for about six months.

Henry and I spent many sessions (when he was awake) trying to understand the meaning of this rather bizarre behavior. It became clear that in addition to the anger expressed by his falling asleep and thereby dismissing and negating me, there was a distinct defensive quality to this behavior. It reminded me of the anecdotes of children in some African tribes who fall asleep when they anticipate being scolded. Most important, in this behavior Henry was reenacting with me, over and over again, the scene of his childhood when his father died prior to their fishing trip. Henry fell "dead" asleep on my couch, and I was forced to revive him and bring him back to life. In this process I too died—I was gone and I disappeared. When he woke up or I awakened him we were reunited after we had temporarily died.

The tragic and traumatic event at age eight—an event that he slept through (as he was "sleeping through life")—was reawakened in his relationship to me. He was reliving that which he could not allow himself to remember by reenacting it with me. In the safety of our intense therapeutic relationship, he was also repeating and repeating this overwhelming event of childhood in an effort to master that which he could not deal with at age eight. In his life he similarly felt he was half asleep during exciting and emotion-laden events—he "didn't get it." Such "sleepwalking" shielded and protected him from experiences that might have been too stimulating and disruptive. Life events that might have made him happy or sad—all melted together and turned "gray." Henry said he felt "dead" and that something and someone were missing in his life.

The "someone" who was missing, led us to spend many hours and many months talking about his father. Slowly as he was able to remember more about the times before his father died he recalled how much he wanted to be like him and yet how distant and silent his father had been. Henry began sobbing when he tried to recall the night his father died—and yet he was certain that he slept through the night of his death. He mostly recalled how disappointed he was when they could not go fishing and he recalled how angry he was when his mother told him he and his father would never go fishing. He also stated that he felt afraid of his mother now that his father was not around. He was not sure what frightened him, but he recalled his uneasiness the first night they were alone. The intense emotionality and the tears that rolled down his face during these sessions was unusual for Henry and after an hour where he cried he would often end our session asking, "What's come over me? Why am I crying? I never cry."

The themes and patterns evoked in examining his sleeping in my office appeared to have been understood and partially resolved, but then reappeared in the analytic material in a different form, and was reworked and reexamined over and over again. His defensive pattern of sleeping or putting others to sleep reemerged in the early part of the third year of our work. Unexpectedly, I found it increasingly difficult to listen to Henry. What he talked about became repetitious, detailed, and totally boring. He talked on and on in great and excessive detail about his job and some of the personnel with whom he worked. I found my thoughts drifting away from the material, and it was hard to "stay with" Henry. This was atypical for me with patients in general and unusual in my previous work with Henry. My distraction alerted me that something was going on between Henry and me but I could not quite see what it was. He then came in and told me he had had a dream and launched into telling me the dream. The dream was in several sections, with many different scenes, multiple characters, and an overwhelming number of details.

The entire session was filled with relating his dream, and there was no time in our session to explore the themes or meaning of this dream. As the hour ended I felt worn out and lost by the flow and quantity of the material—it felt endless and confusing. It then occurred to me that Henry was trying to hypnotize me or put me to sleep or get rid of me. I felt excluded and cut adrift as our meeting ended.

The following day, Henry again started by telling me details about his job—who ran what system, the personalities of some of his coworkers, and time schedules. I interrupted this flow and said "Henry, I've been thinking about the material from the last few weeks, the job, the coworkers, schedules and then that very complicated dream from yesterday which we did not have time to talk about—and I have some sense that you are trying to push me out of this room, or somehow turn on the fog machine (an expression we had used in the past to refer to defenses he used to 'not see things')." Henry was angry, and he said he was "furious with me." He said, "You tell me to say whatever comes to my mind. I do that and now you're telling me that it's not good enough." Henry raged on a while longer about my insensitivity and contradictory messages. I then said, "well you make a good point about confusing messages, but what I am saying is that what is coming to your mind in the last few weeks—details about your work—is a way to keep me out of the room and to keep other things on your mind—out of your thinking." There was a very long silence and Henry started, "I began to see Karen (a girl he had casually met at work)—and I asked her out for a date, and it did not go well, and I felt humiliated". Henry then went on to tell me that after many months of hesitation he had asked a young women coworker out to dinner. They started meeting on some regular basis, and on her instigation they ended up in her apartment and in her bed. He was unable to have an erection. She was critical and teasing and he felt "totally destroyed and humiliated " This occurred about a week before Henry started to tell me the many details about work. He felt he could not let himself think about or talk about his feelings of humiliation—that in itself would have been humiliating. Henry had suffered a similar experience as an adolescent with his one girlfriend, and as a result avoided all dating for ten years.

As we explored the situation, Henry recalled that after his father died, his mother continued to "lose it"—that is, have outbursts of temper regularly. In addition she often sought out Henry as someone to help her with her loneliness and depression. She would ask him to join her in her bed because she was unable to sleep. Though Henry enjoyed this attention, he also experienced great discomfort and anxiety associated with this new intimacy. After several months of sharing his mother's bed he refused to stay in her room. His mother became angry and stopped talking to him for two weeks.

Henry had tried to keep all of this material, the memories, the humiliating experience out of his and my view by his "fog machine," so neither of us could see what was going on in his mind. This "walling off" of these emotionally charged memories and feelings was similar to how he isolated the experiences of this father's death by remaining asleep. As Henry and I talked about these memories and early enmeshment with his mother, it became clear that these experiences were directly related to Henry's current difficulties with intimacy with women, and this became an area for much exploration and for Henry's further experimentations with dating and closeness.

In the fourth year of our work, I sensed Henry's intense effort to mimic and identify with me. For instance I noticed that he bought eyeglasses that looked just like mine. Some words and phrases that I tended to use—I heard echoed back to me. He began asking questions about my personal life—where I went to school and what kind of car I drove. As we examined this effort to imitate and then identify with me, Henry began to talk about the intense rage he had toward his father for never being a father and not protecting him from the out-of-control tantrums of his mother. He remembered yearning to be like his father—but father always remained so aloof and unavailable. And then father totally disappeared through death. This was the ultimate loss and abandonment. A reflection of Henry's loss and anger was expressed in how little he remembered about his father. He had very little memory of him and found the photos of his father to be bewildering. He was a stranger. In his rage Henry had obliterated his father from his memory. In this way Henry remained aloof and abandoned by his father. He never mentioned his father and if I asked—he had only a vague sense of who his father was and if he really existed. Beneath this rage we discovered the deep yearning for a father figure who would protect him, mentor him, and serve as a role model. He suffered dearly from "father hunger." His attempts to mimic and identify with me represented this profound wish and futile attempt to fill this childhood void. As we came to explore this part of his inner life, Henry became disappointed in me for indeed I could not fill the emptiness he felt. I could not live up to the childhoodidealized image he had created of me. I, like his father let him down. If there was some confusion about appointment schedules, he became distressed and angry with me as if I had failed some sort of test. If I forgot a name he had mentioned in passing, or if I seemed not to understand a point he was making, Henry experienced such "errors" on my part as abandonments and that I was not fully in touch with him. From his perspective I had left him and gone on a "business trip."

The analysis lasted a little over five years and allowed Henry to "wake up" and to more fully experience and participate in the world around him. At first this reawakening became apparent and was played out in the analytic sessions. Whereas in our early years together all his feelings were muted and hidden behind an intellectual and gray facade, as our time together continued, he was able to be far more emotional and alive. He could sob and cry when talking about his father whom he hardly knew and could rage at me when he felt I was letting him down. Then his life outside the office began to be much more colorful. He and two associates at work decided to leave the large firm and set-up their own group. The venture was exciting and successful. His work blossomed and became "interesting" and remarkably profitable. He developed a strong and loving relationship with a young woman (the first in his life) and this helped fill some of the emptiness that lingered. Though Henry worked long hours, he decided to do some volunteer work in the community and joined the local EMT (emergency medical technician) group and was often called in the middle of the night to help revive a stricken victim. He found this exciting and felt that he was making a meaningful contribution.

Henry comments

The most striking aspect of this narrative and the treatment process was Henry's enactment and reliving with me the trauma of his father's sudden death. For about six months, on an almost daily basis, Henry fell "dead" asleep on my couch. Though Henry had no conscious memory of being in bed with his father when his father suffered a massive heart attack—Henry remained asleep—it became clear that this nonremembered trauma became an enduring part of his internal life. The trauma was not remembered but it was indelible.

This indelible dynamic was reflected in two ways:

1. *It was dramatically enacted with me in my office. Within the regressive and intense analytic relationship (and lying on the couch) the events of the night that his father died were rekindled. The scene that he could not remember was played out in the here and now with me. Day after day he "died" on my couch, and I had to "revive" him. In a parallel way I repeatedly faded away (I died), and when he woke up I was again quite alive. In this way we were repeating over and over again the loss through the sudden death, but a wishful element was added—death became a "big sleep" and one wakes up from death (a common childhood conception).*

   Trauma, either acute or chronic, can distort and disrupt memory and the traumatic events can be obliterated from memory. Expressed more fully, the trauma can be so overwhelming to the psyche and the neurobiological system that the memory of the trauma is split off, sequestered, walled off or stored in the mind in a way that it is not retrievable through recollection. Though the individual's emotional equilibrium is thereby protected from being overwhelmed, there is a price to be paid in the discontinuity of experience and in that the trauma endures and becomes an unconscious dynamic factor in ongoing development.

2. *The second reflection of the nonremembered traumatic memory is more subtle and yet far more significant in Henry's personality formation. Just as Henry was able to remain asleep during the chaos of his father's heart attack, and thereby block the experience from awareness, Henry defensively cut himself off from the vicissitudes of life—,*

the joys, sorrows, the struggles and the intimacies of existence that threatened to arouse him and thereby upset his emotional equilibrium. He did this by isolating himself, avoiding contacts and muting his daily experiences. As he expressed it, "I'm half-asleep. I seem to be missing life—I don't get it—I'm just passing through." Life was gray and colorless—he sensed it—, it troubled him and he came to therapy to find better solutions.

An example of this muting or avoiding life could be seen in his relationship to women. In high school he dated a girl once or twice and felt "awkward and very uncomfortable." He then did not go out with a woman for the next ten years. When finally a woman coworker seduced him into her bedroom, he recalled feeling aroused but then almost overwhelmed with anxiety. "I had to curb my enthusiasm." He suddenly found himself worrying about the unfinished work he left on his desk and as a result he was unable to sustain an erection.

A good deal of our analytic work was to clarify, confront, reconstruct, and understand his need to remain half-asleep in life and how this related to his protecting himself and not being aroused by the trauma of his father's death. Gradually there was an "awakening"—at first in the safety of the analytic relationship. He began to express profound sadness about the things he was missing in life and then a sense of outrage at his father for never showing him "how to be a man" and how his father did nothing to stop "that crazy woman." He became disappointed with me and then quite angry with me when he failed "to be a man" with the woman who tried to seduce him. I failed him and therapy failed him. Gradually he then allowed himself to be awake in his daily life—he became entrepreneurial and successful in his work, and he developed an intimate and fulfilling relationship with a young woman.

Most things in an individual's emotional life do not develop de novo—there are developmental antecedents and roots to what we see unfolding. The trauma occurring with his father's tragic death and the defensive or coping path into which Henry moved had a context. Even before his father's death, Henry's mother was described as labile, emotionally immature, and prone to unpredictable temper tantrums. Henry felt terrified of her and her "moods." His father remained aloof and uninvolved. He would not or could not modulate her behavior or protect his son. Henry coped with this situation by himself withdrawing, like his father, and he was characterized as shy, inhibited, and removed. So in fact, Henry was figuratively already using his "half-asleep" defenses to deal with a difficult life situation. Then his father had a massive heart attack—a trauma that threatened to overwhelm this eight-year-old child. Now Henry literally stayed asleep and totally withdrew from the event—and then emotionally withdrew from life.

Henry's volunteer work was very important to him. He was dedicated and deeply involved with this activity. Unlike the eight-year-old child who was passively subjected to an overwhelming trauma, in his volunteer work as an EMT worker he actively confronted life-anddeath scenes. When he was on call, a siren in his home woke him, and he rushed to rescue and revive the stricken victim. He was proud and fully immersed in this heroic activity.

5

Mary—
An unfulfilled life

L ike a sandstorm, Mary blew into my psychotherapeutic practice, blinded me, caused disruption, and then disappeared.

I returned a call from a woman asking to see me in consultation. I asked her who had referred her and she indicated Paul from the university health center. Though it was a little unusual that Paul had not called me in advance to ask about my available time, however, I knew him well and neglecting this important bit of protocol was not atypical for him. Paul had been a student of mine several years back—and I agreed to set up an appointment with Mary—the woman on the phone. I proceeded to call Paul but was informed by his secretary that he was out of town.

Mary was a forty-year-old woman who was very attractive, well dressed, personable, and articulate. She had recently completed a master's degree program in linguistics at the local university and had seen Paul at the student health center.

I found it a little difficult to ascertain why she was seeing me or why Paul had referred her. She seemed evasive about the details. Mary indicated that she had been a little depressed several months ago, but meeting with Paul was helpful, and she was no longer depressed. I inquired why she was not continuing to work with Paul since it sounded like their meetings had been helpful. Mary responded, somewhat coquettishly, that she and Paul were having some difficulties and "he suggested I see you in consultation."

To describe some context for this consultation, a few words about Paul are in order. I knew Paul fairly well. He had finished his psychiatric training about four years before my meeting with Mary, and Paul was now working in the student health center. He periodically asked me to see a student in consultation. I had been one of his teachers / supervisors while he was in training and our work went well. Paul was a very handsome man— of movie star quality. He was bright, creative, personable, and talented. He was considered by the faculty as somewhat of a "rebel" in that he questioned and objected to many of the training program policies. Some of his suggestions were helpful, others were just challenging. As his supervisor on occasion I had to question his judgment about setting boundaries with his patients. He had a somewhat seductive style with his attractive female patients, and I thought this might someday cause him grief. Paul was now married with two young children, but I had recently heard that he was having some marital difficulties. Thus the scene was set for my encounter with Mary.

After my first meeting with Mary, I called Paul at his office and then at home to learn more about this consultation, and I learned that he was in Europe for a monthlong vacation.

During my second evaluative meeting with Mary I pressed further about why she was seeing me. With a slightly embarrassed smile Mary said that she and Paul were planning to get married. He was leaving his wife, and he and Mary were to be married the following spring. Mary had not been married before, she had always lived by herself, and she said that Paul thought it would be helpful if she have some premarital counseling and suggested that she see me. I was a little taken aback and annoyed. I was not pleased to be involved in this situation. I considered myself a friend of Paul's wife, and I did not like the role assigned to me, that is, to prepare this woman as a replacement wife.

I had scheduled to meet with Mary for a third evaluative interview before I was to leave for my two-week summer vacation. During this meeting I obtained some limited background information. Mary had two older brothers and added, "I was a surprise to my elderly parents." The family lived in a small midwestern city and was involved in farming. The family life was described as, "pleasant and peaceful." Though her parents were very "silent" and retiring, Mary was close to her brothers. She reported having a very quiet life in her small town and she enjoyed her school years. Mary attended a local college and dated and hoped to marry one of her teachers—but "that did not work out". She worked for a few years at the community newspaper but her social life was "dull." Her father died and her mother moved to a local retirement village. Her two brothers with their families continued to work the farm. Mary enjoyed her nieces and nephews— but felt disappointed that she did not have children of her own. Mary moved to an eastern city and attended the university where she earned her master's degree in linguistics. Though she hoped that the move would introduce her to a fuller social life, she lived alone, and she made very few friends. Several months prior to our consultation, Mary began having menopausal symptoms. She indicated that the realization that she would never have children saddened her and she sought help at the student health clinic for her depression and was assigned to Paul.

In this third meeting I sensed something was unusual about this woman, but I was not sure exactly what it was. She was articulate and appeared thoughtful, but no matter what we talked about—her unhappiness in growing up, her disappointment in her current social life, her sense of isolation at the university—she seemed constantly to be smiling—an enigmatic smile. I assumed she was pleased about her upcoming marriage. However, I still was not clear why she was seeing me.

I met with Mary my first day back from my vacation. Again she had her "Mona Lisa" smile, and I asked her about her smile since it puzzled me. She said she was very happy to see me. I also noticed that she had taken her shoes off when she sat on the soft chair opposite me.

Later that day I was finally able to reach Paul, and he told me he had seen Mary for about three months and she had become totally delusional about plans to marry him. Paul reported that Mary could not be budged from this belief, and he felt he had reached an impossible impasse with her. He remembered that in his training years I had helped him with a few situations that became "sticky," and he hoped I could be of help to him by seeing her in consultation. He said he was "very, very sorry" he had not called me in advance about the referral—but he was caught up in arrangements for his monthlong trip with his family. "Sorry" he again repeated.

At our next meeting I told Mary about my conversation with Paul. She smiled and said with little hesitation that the real plan, and why she was seeing me, was that she knew that she was going to marry *me* in the spring. She was certain that Paul and I had worked this out.

Over the next four months Mary and I talked about her ideas and her conviction about our relationship. I tried to explore with her the depression, and disappointments that she wished to rectify in her life situation. I told her that though her wishes were understandable, it distorted our real relationship and would inevitably end with another disappointment. She seemed unable to step back and hear this. Mary continued to smile and thanked me for my concern. She knew that in my way I was trying to prepare her for our marriage—and she was very grateful.

I continued to meet with her twice weekly and continued to try to get her to step back and look at her belief system and the scenario she had created as a way to deal with her disappointments in life, but it was clear that she could not do this. Her ideas and wishfulfilling delusions were "fixed." She smiled at my comments and my efforts to get her to examine her thoughts and feelings.

Mary then became increasingly intrusive in my life. She somehow was able to learn my home address and the number of children I had and their names. She sent me a variety of letters that were undecipherable, and a series of packages with old clothing and useless trinkets. When I met with her and asked her about these things she indicated she thought we could use these items in our future home. The toys were meant for "our" children. On several occasions she pounded on my office door while I was seeing other patients and indignantly demanded to know what time was I picking her up for dinner. To those around her, Mary seemed quite normal. She was quite articulate and could be rather charming. Her apparent "normality" was sufficient to cause me grief in the small suburban community where I lived. I received calls from local merchants to approve some purchases "Mrs. Fischer" was making. The local police found her loitering, and they called me to pick "Mrs. Fischer" up from the station.

Trying to prescribe some antipsychotic medication for her was useless. She saw no need for this. She had no family within a thousand miles, and she had no friends in the area. I asked her to voluntarily enter the hospital for some testing and more intensive treatment but this was rejected as "silly and unnecessary." She was not legally committable—since she had not made any attempts to harm herself or anyone else—though I was becoming concerned that she knew where my family lived and the names of my children. Her elderly mother called me from the midwest and wondered if it was true that there was to be a spring wedding. Finally on a bright and brisk winter Saturday morning I saw a very large rental truck come up the long and narrow driveway of my home and crushing the shrubbery. Mary was driving and she had packed up all her furniture and possessions and was preparing to move into my home. I had to call the local police to remove her and her truck from my property. The police were able to keep her in custody for three days on charges of trespassing.

During this time I contacted Mary's mother in her midwest retirement village and then spoke with the two older brothers who came east to pick up their baby sister.

I was able to keep contact with her brothers for the next year by phone. Mary became seriously suicidal when she was home and had to be hospitalized. When I last spoke to them they reported that Mary had been out on leave from the hospital and died in a car accident that they thought she had caused.

I felt very sad about a life lost.

Mary comments

Eliciting a fuller picture of Mary's life before she developed her delusional system would have been helpful and allowed for a deeper appreciations of the factors that led to the presenting clinical picture. Illnesses such as Mary's, except perhaps in cases of severe trauma, do not evolve de novo—there is almost always some prior dysfunction or maladaptive patterns of behavior that precede and set the stage for the immediate disorder. However, Mary was deeply enmeshed in her delusional system when she came for "marriage counseling," and it became clear that she did not want to look back and think about the past—a past that she experienced as " dull, unproductive, and wasted." She felt pleasure and comfort in focusing on the future that in her wish-fulfilling fantasies was to be happy and filled with good things such as companionship and children. Indeed Mary maintained her "Mona Lisa" smile in her effort to keep this joyful scenario alive in her mind. As the weeks passed and her delusional system remained fixed, it became apparent that much darker forces were threatening to erupt. Suicidal thoughts were not spoken, but I believe they lingered in her mind. Her menopausal symptoms may well have confronted her with the disappointments of her past, the uncertainties of her future and the rapid passage of time.

Though the "remedy" and solution to her emotional pain were delusional and ultimately led to collapse and further depression, Mary's illness is understandable in terms of an appreciation of the human condition. Mary was very sad and depressed about her life as it had so far unfolded. In a moment of sadness she complained that she had "wasted so many years." I became increasingly apparent that Mary did not have the internal resources to find more adaptive ways to struggle with these disappointments, and she created in her mind a future and a delusional world based on her wishes and dreams.

If one thinks of "normality" and serious psychological dysfunction on a spectrum, it is not difficult to understand some of the mental processes that led to Mary's illness and how such dynamic factors are very much part of the human condition. Mary's depression and her feeling that she had wasted her years and then her grim uncertainty about the future are issues that are not emotional strangers, and for many people the developmental tasks associated with the middle years of live are considered a normal "midlife crises." Heightened self-reflections, looking back and looking forward at this time in the life cycle can hopefully lead to new directions and new creativity. For some however, like Mary, such self-reflection may result in a level of existential despair and uncertainty—and result in dysfunctional compromises.

The use of fantasy, dreams, and a tincture of self-deception are not uncommon ways humans deal with difficult life situations. In optimal circumstances such dreaming and planning may lead to growthful and imaginative thinking and actions. In children who understandably may feel small and weak, playing "make-believe" and enacting their fantasies of being a princess or a superhero, may be temporarily useful, developmentally expected and considered "charming." However, when children play "make-believe" and are then confronted with the reality that it is time for dinner, they know that their dramatic persona is in fact "make-believe."

Mary's illness represented a level of dysfunction near the far end of the mental health spectrum. For her, her fantasies were not fantasies they were wished-for realities. The scenarios she was trying to live out were not "make-believe"—they were her realities. Though her actions and behavior took on a bizarre quality when viewed by the outside observer, her struggles, pain, and her attempts at coping with a life situation that she felt was despairing and hopeless—were not alien to the human condition. For reasons buried in her earlier life experiences and perhaps in her biology, Mary was propelled into a flight from reality. Ultimately this flight resulted in tragedy.

In the Introduction and in many of the clinical examples in this book, the importance of an emotional immersion is underscored as an important part of insight-oriented psychotherapy. Such immersion and emotional involvement provides a here and now immediacy that make confrontation and exploration have greater impact and meaning. In Mary's case her immersion became a submersion and a delusional experience. She did not have sufficient internal resources to appreciate that her connection to her therapists were wish-fulfilling fantasies. For her it was not an "as if" experience rather it was her all absorbing reality, and as such she had to live out her reality rather than being able to stand back and with the therapist examine the experience and expand her understanding of herself.

6

Sara—
"I'm afraid I will Kill my infant"

"I 'm afraid I will kill my daughter. She was born a month ago."
This fear, a fear that was almost paralytic, was the reason why Sara came to see me for consultation. This was her first child—planned and much desired. Soon after birth, however, she began having thoughts that she might by accident or intent kill the infant girl. Such thoughts were particularly prominent when her newborn daughter cried, and Sara felt helpless and did not know what to do. She felt terrified by her own murderous thoughts and horrified and panicked by such thinking. She was especially uneasy when she was alone with the baby and insisted that a nanny or her husband remain with her when she was feeding the infant.

Sara was thirty-two years old when we first met. She was an attractive, articulate, and intelligent woman. She seemed introspective and sensitive. Sara had been married several years before the pregnancy and was looking forward to motherhood.

Sara had been thinking of seeing a psychiatrist for many years prior to this acute state of panic but felt that psychotherapy would be too much of a self-indulgence. For as long as she could remember she felt "tied down," "depressed," "half-alive," "dull," "unproductive,""inhibited," and somehow "hiding from life." Sara had no idea why she felt this way, but she knew she was unhappy and thought having a child would help her feel better. During the pregnancy she felt happy and even mildly euphoric. Now, one month after the baby was born, she felt terrified of her thoughts and panicked that she might lose control and kill her infant.

Sara and I began meeting twice a week to try to explore and understand her current acute panic as well as her lifelong feelings of depression and inadequacy. In my initial evaluation it seemed that Sara's acute difficulties, her fear of harming her baby, were very closely tied to her chronic lifelong depression and inhibition. I sensed that her current crisis represented a decompensation of her more chronic but stabilized dysfunction.

Sara was a much-desired firstborn child. Her parents, both professionals, were married for five years before Sara's birth. Early development was reported to have been "normal" and unfolded without difficulty. What stood out in her early history and that was particularly relevant in terms of the current crisis was that at age five a sister was born. When this infant was six months old, she contracted an infectious illness and spent many hours each day and night in anguished crying. The parents were distraught and seemed helpless, and Sara was terrified and hid beneath her bed to muffle the awful screeching. Then when the infant was eight months old she died. Though Sara's memories were fragmentary, she remembered feeling somehow responsible for her sister's death and the subsequent family sadness. She had wished for the sister to stop howling, "it was so terrible," and for her parents to turn their attention back to her. Then her sister did stop crying and it was a great relief. However, Sara's world turned gray.

Sara's parents became deeply depressed and they remained silent in their grief. They never mentioned the dead child, and tried to act as if she never existed. Sara, who was filled with fantasies, guilt, and bewilderment, watched as her parents became more and more silent and increasingly more withdrawn and inaccessible. As the years passed the home continued to be a "house of mourning"—somber and joyless. The dead sister was never mentioned. Sara's mother became more absorbed in herself and her career, and her father developed a series of undiagnosed somatic complaints and chronic fatigue. Of particular distress to Sara was when she would talk to him about school decisions and social worries, often his eyes would close, and he appeared to fall asleep. Sara commented, "I thought he wasn't interested in me. I guess he was just depressed."

Though talented and well trained, Sara's scholastic and career efforts were muted. She felt she was not particularly talented and had great difficulty developing her skills. She described feeling as if she were "always trying to drive a car in neutral." Her teachers often commented that she had great potential, but she never seemed to excel or allow herself to be creative. Her mentors were often disappointed in her work. She married a college classmate whom she described as affectionate and intelligent, and for the most part the marriage seemed to be fulfilling and harmonious. Her husband felt irritated with Sara during her periods of depression—depressions that might last for days, weeks, or months. He noted that their lives were filled with good things, their relationship was comfortable, and there was no reason for her to be sad.

In our early work together we focused our attention on her feelings of panic when she was caring for her infant daughter. Though it was clear that the newborn child reactivated the buried memories and fears that surrounded the trauma of her sister's death, this was a startling revelation for Sara. She was surprised and even stunned when I pointed out the obvious parallels and connections. Just as her parents could not talk about the dead infant, Sara could not let herself think about her dead sister and her guilt about "causing" the tragedy. She sobbed as she recalled her loneliness when her sister died twenty years earlier. At the time her parents were too depressed to help her with her despair and to help her clarify her imagined responsibility. In fact their silence, and their inability to successfully mourn their loss, increased Sara's isolation and feelings of responsibility. For months in her therapy she spoke with great sadness about those terrible times when her sister stopped screaming—times she was discouraged from speaking about and even thinking about. As Sara began to see and struggle with her buried memories and distortions of childhood and how these "demons" were haunting her life, her anxieties surrounding her own infant began to melt away. Her panic attacks disappeared and she came to fully enjoy her daughter. It was no longer her sister who was "howling"— rather it was her infant daughter who needed some attention.

Sara was no longer in acute distress, but her lifelong struggle with chronic depression and the inhibition of her creative talents that were draining her life of color were much more difficult and complicated to address. Though she was quite talented and able, Sara could not let herself be successful or to flourish. Her teachers saw this throughout her school career. She was constantly told that she was not "living up to her potential." Sara felt that she was "second-rate" and that she deserved being ignored and overlooked. To be successful and to excel was not part of how she saw herself, and yet she resented and became angry and depressed when she was "left in the shadows." When her husband took on a new and interesting job—she felt neglected and her depression reemerged. When a friend became preoccupied with a personal family matter, Sara felt excluded and hurt. When her child was born and took center stage, Sara felt pushed to the background, and this added to her depression.

These more chronic aspects of Sara's character structure—her negative self-image, her sensitivity to being "ignored," and her inability to realize her potential—could be understood as deriving from the traumatic events surrounding and following her sister's death. In her mind, as a five-year-old child, Sara had indeed been successful in quieting and ridding herself of her disruptive sister. The omnipotence and magical thinking of childhood provided the background for such a fantasy formation and distortion. Her parents were unable to help her or even allow themselves to be aware of her feelings and correct these distortions. They themselves were depleted by the loss. Their depression and withdrawal served to confirm Sara's sense of responsibility. As Sara and I explored these issues, it became clear that her feelings of loss and guilt were not recognized and certainly were not addressed. She and her inner world of feelings and "imaginations" were ignored and thereby relegated to the "unimportant" and to be forgotten or at least not spoken. Her mother's increasing activity outside the home as her way of coping with her own sadness was experienced by Sara as evidence that her inner distress was "trivial" and to be ignored. Her father's falling asleep when she told him her worries served to confirm this self-perception.

As a child, Sara was a very good child and in fact she tried to be the perfect child. In adolescence she never rebelled, complained, or asserted herself. Throughout these years she was unconsciously trying to "make it up" to her chronically depressed parents. In her magical thinking she had harmed them and was trying to "make amends" and even trying to "treat" their depressions by being the perfect child. As noted earlier in her school years she remained a shy, retiring, and "good" girl, but it was clear to her teachers that her work fell far below her potential. This pattern continued as she pursued her career. She could not allow herself to use her native talents and grow. Though she resented and was hurt by being in the shadows and overlooked, this also provided her with a "safe place," and a place to be ignored. To be assertive and to imagine and wish for success carried with it certain unconscious dangers as evidenced by the fulfillment of her wish that her sister stop crying.

Many of these themes and internal conflicts became alive and part of our therapeutic sessions. Sara tried to be the perfect patient by agreeing with everything I said, and I often had to confront her about this blind compliance. I commented, "Sara, by always agreeing with whatever I say, you are really ignoring me and what I am saying. I wonder if you are telling me how you sometimes feel when you believe you are merely being tolerated but sense that you are really being ignored." This comment both confused her and frustrated her. She cried, "What do you want from me? Do you want me to argue with you and say you are wrong—I'll do that if you want!! I want you to like me. I don't want to cause you trouble." We talked and explored her response in terms of not wanting to cause her depressed parents any more trouble . "Losing their child, my sister, was too much for them already. I had to be good to make it up to them—whatever the cost to me."

Also in our sessions, it became clear how sensitive and responsive Sara was if she felt not listened to or ignored. Prior to one particular therapy hour I was informed on the phone of a personal family health problem. Sara quickly sensed that I was not totally with her in the session and that my mind had wandered away from her. She became sullen and quiet, and I asked her what had happened between us. With great reluctance she said that she felt I had left the office, and I was not really listening to her. I acknowledged that she was correct and that I had become distracted by a personal family matter. We then proceeded to examine what this felt like and what this meant to her. It was like her father falling asleep when she told him about her worries and her husband being preoccupied with his new job. Her response found roots in her being ignored when her sister died and her parents were unable to hear her turmoil and anguish. She felt immediately pushed into the shadows and ignored. Her pain was unimportant. Rather than protest when I was not attentive to her, Sara withdrew, felt worthless and depressed. This was a central dynamic in the here and now of our session and it was a key struggle to be explored and understood. It also became clear how this pattern characterized many of her relationships to friends and family and often led her into depressive patterns of behavior that further isolated her from those whom she needed most.

Sara's course in therapy took a somewhat unique path. Our psychotherapeutic relationship continued for nearly thirty years. Her pattern was that she would see me two or three times a week for about two years and then indicate she would like to see how things were going without active treatment. Then for periods of three to four years she would not come to my office but would send me letters several times a year relating how her life was unfolding and also about the many things she had been thinking about and discovering in her self-analytic activities. Her observations and insights were usually quite perceptive, sensitive, and proved to be helpful. I would send back brief notes, commenting on her observations and thoughts.

As I followed her for nearly thirty years, it was clear that Sara's life had expanded and had become rich and rewarding. She was a warm and loving mother to her daughter and then had a second child, a son, several years latter without difficulty and with much joy. Her career blossomed, and she was creative and successful in her work. She occasionally had periods of depression and feelings that she was "stagnating" in life, and it was this that motivated her to call me for an appointment. We might then resume meeting on a regular basis for a year of two until she wanted to see how things went on her own.

Sara comments

I will comment on four aspect of this case: (1) the acute and chronic phases of Sara's dysfunction, (2) when trauma becomes traumatic, (3) enhanced self-analytic functioning, and (4) an in vivo or transferential component in this case.

1. *Sara had come to live with and accept her chronic personality dysfunction. She and many of those around her were aware that she was shy, inhibited, did not live up to her potential, periodically became depressed, and was easily hurt in her interpersonal relationships. She did very little to remedy these restrictions on her life because she felt to seek help (psychotherapy) would be "self indulgent." Of course this reluctance to get help for herself was part of her personality structure and her feeling that she was not deserving of attention and should be ignored. Such a level of personality dysfunction for many people in our society often remains unattended to and merely plays itself out in a lifelong pattern of unhappiness or a sense of being "unfulfilled."*

   The birth of her baby and the rekindling of memories of her sister's death shifted her emotional equilibrium and her habitual techniques of coping with her inner conflicts, no longer worked and she became acutely symptomatic. She was terrified that she might kill her newborn infant (as she imagined she killed her sister) and her panic pressed her to seek treatment. One can assume that if she had not developed her acute symptoms she would never have had the opportunity of addressing and treating the underlying character disorder and the depression that were in fact draining the color and joy from her life.

Sara's acute symptoms (panic) were ameliorated within the first six months of treatment when she was able to see and understand how the memories of her own childhood trauma were overwhelming her current life experiences. The more deeply embedded character dysfunction and her chronic depression, however, required a much longer time to understand and ultimately change. In our present societal setting, where McTherapy is an accepted model, it would have been easy for Sara and her therapist to stop treatment when her acute symptoms abated and ignore the personality dysfunction as she and her parents had done for so many years. It was a level of dysfunction that she had come to live with, though it was clearly to her detriment.

2. *The death of her sister when Sara was five years old was a very traumatic life event. Most children would have been deeply troubled by such misfortune. However, we must ask why this terrible happening laid the groundwork for her lifelong personality dysfunction and her chronic depression. I would suggest that it was the context and the surrounding events that made this loss become an enduring element that so profoundly influenced her developing personality. This five-year-old child had no one to help her process her grief and loss, and no one to*

*help her unravel the reality and her distorted sense that
she was responsible for the sadness that descended on her
family. Sara's parents were themselves unable to
satisfactorily grieve and cope with their loss, and in their
withdrawal they left Sara alone with her own feelings and
distortions. Indeed, her parents' withdrawal and
abandonment served to add to Sara's burden and her
sense that she had done some terrible deed for which she
deserved to be punished and abandoned. These events set
the stage for a trauma evolving into a lifelong
preoccupation.*

3. *One of the principle goals in psychoanalytic therapy is for
the analysand to develop or enhance their self-analytic
abilities so that they are better able to utilize the tools of
the treatment experience for further insight and growth.
Self-reflection and an appreciation of the dynamics of
one's inner world are essential in this process. This
function had clearly developed with Sara. When Sara was
not actively seeing me she wrote me notes regularly about
the things she observed, thought about, and had learned
about herself through her self-analytic work. Sara found
such insights very helpful in her interpersonal
relationships and in her life.*

4. *Sara's ability to confront me (though reluctantly) when
my thoughts had wandered out of the treatment situation
was an important opportunity for us to explore. This
experience of "abandonment" was a central issue in her
childhood and was carried into her adult life and very
much influenced her interpersonal relationships. As a five-
year-old child her parents, because of their own grief, had
abandoned her to her own inner turmoil, guilt, and
distortions. She felt alone and "ignored." As an adult she*

remained vigilant and highly sensitive to when she felt "overlooked" and when this happened she was angered and then withdrew and typically became depressed and self-deprecating. This in turn added to her isolation and loneliness. In confronting me and my acknowledging her perception and then our going on to explore what this meant to her, we had an in vivo *experience, that we could explore and better understand. It was a palpable and emotion-filled encounter. The impact of confronting and exploring it as a here and now moment greatly added to the impact of her understanding. It was not an abstraction or an historical event we were talking about— it was an alive, powerful, palpable event that was "in our face." The awareness of this pattern, the expansion of our understanding of this dynamic, and an appreciation of the roots of her hypersensitivity proved most helpful in Sara's relationships to those around her.*

7

Diana—
Self-loathing as a core belief

My treatment of Diana was a failure—indeed a failure that proved to be fatal. I present this case because it sheds some light on important aspects of human development and the human condition. The case also underscores the limitations of psychotherapy.

I learned about Diana from her previous therapist. He asked me to see if I could work with this young woman. Diana had been in treatment with several therapists previously. My referring colleague indicated that he had tried for several years to engage Diana in a therapeutic relationship but felt they had made no progress and sadly commented, "I feel totally drained by Diana, and I don't think I am being helpful." This therapist was a friend whom I considered competent and sensitive. Such referrals however, are often fraught with difficulty.

Diana was a second born child. Her brother was fifteen years her senior. The parents were older and clearly Diana's conception was not planned or desired. The pregnant mother was distraught and demanded to have an abortion. The family's religious convictions and strong pressure from the husband and the family priest made this option unacceptable. While pregnant with Diana, her mother had several "accidents," such as falling down the steps and fracturing her wrist, and subsequently suffering a concussion after a second fall. She was not successful in "accidently" aborting the fetus.

Diana's mother had a serious problem with alcohol for many years before Diana was born and her drinking escalated after the birth. She became seriously depressed during the postpartum period and in the first several years after Diana was born she spent about half of her time away from home—in psychiatric facilities, in rehabilitation programs, or just disappearing and secluding herself in a hotel or a rented room. Often she could not be located for several days. Diana's care was managed by a series of nurses and housekeepers. Even when mother was home, she had difficulty relating to her infant daughter. Diana's father, a successful industrialist, watched but apparently felt unable to intervene other than paying for staff to care for his daughter when his wife was absent. The older brother was heavily using street drugs and soon after graduating from high school moved to California and disappeared from the family.

Diana had many early memories of her parents fighting— usually when her mother had been drinking. She recalled the battles being violent, physical, loud, and terrifying. Many of the fights seemed related to Diana, such as, who would care for her, who should provide discipline, and who was responsible for her existence. Diana often imagined that someone would be killed in these fights and remembered wondering when her mother disappeared if she was dead or if she would ever return.

When Diana was eight years old, her mother committed suicide by overdosing with pills and alcohol. Diana recalls feeling "numb" and a kind of "nothingness." She wasn't sure what had happened but recalls some relief that there were no more fights at home. She also recalls a sense that she was somehow responsible for her mother going away because she had been a "naughty girl." Her father became quite depressed, and he was unable to return to his office and remained at home. He spent more and more time with Diana, and in retrospect Diana suggested "he was using me like a security blanket." For several months when he was feeling particularly "blue and lonesome" he had Diana sleep with him in his bed. Diana recalls feeling very uneasy in this situation and thought something was wrong. At one point she realized that he had an erection when they shared the parents' bed. Though she was uncertain what this meant, she then insisted on moving from the bed to the floor of her parents' bedroom.

Eight months after the suicide, Diana's father returned to work but then absented himself from the home and his daughter. He worked long hours, socialized, and traveled on weekends and saw Diana rarely. A series of housekeepers, nannies, and companions were hired. No one lasted more than a few months. Diana was always sad, sullen, angry, and rejecting—and the various caretakers moved on.

Diana's school experience was also rather dismal. She had difficulty making friends, tended to be a loner and rejected classmates and teachers who tried to befriend her. She had outbursts of unprovoked rage, and this further alienated schoolmates. She remembered, "I was always depressed and always angry. No one liked me."

In high school, she learned that an assortment of street drugs made her feel better or at least less lonesome and "empty." By tenth grade she was deeply into using drugs to keep her "afloat." Obtaining money from her father that she then used for drugs was never a problem. She also discovered that by slashing herself with razor blades or glass on her arms, thighs or abdomen, she felt "more real and less empty" and temporarily less depressed.

The school authorities and her father finally insisted Diana see a therapist. She consulted with many therapists but usually the contact was brief. Sometimes Diana would refuse to talk, and there was silence for weeks—until the treatment contact ended. Also, in the several years after she graduated from high school, she had three hospitalizations—primarily related to overdosing with pills. During one of her hospitalizations she was administered twelve electroshock treatments. Besides some temporary memory loss, these treatments had little apparent effect.

When I was asked to consult with Diana she was twenty-four. She had never worked, and her father gave her a very ample allowance to live on. She clearly did not want to see me. Her attire was disheveled and unattractive. She looked like a young "bag lady." She glared at me and was generally contemptuous of my attempts to engage her in conversation or to obtain some basic information. After a series of tense and difficult evaluation sessions, I told her that I planned to meet with her six days a week. Diana was outraged by the frequency of the sessions. I told her that meeting with her less often would not be helpful and that I hoped we could use our time together profitably. Initially she came for her appointments because her father threatened to cut off all her funds if she refused. We met daily for the next four-and-a-half years.

In the early months she worked at trying to get rid of me. She loudly asserted that I was wasting her time and my time. I was seeing her only for her father's money. She spit our disdainfully, "You must be a prostitute . . . You are no better than the other therapists—maybe even worse . . . Why don't you get an honest job?"

Most of my early efforts were trying to clarify and understand her need to drive me away. I commented, "Diana, we both know how lonesome and empty you feel, and yet you are so intent in chasing people and me away. You work to destroy what might be helpful." I wondered out loud about all the people in her life—her mother, her father, schoolmates, and therapists who she felt "bailed out" on her and maybe now she was trying to protect herself by "bailing out" first. Diana tended to ignore my comments or tell me "I was full of crap."

However, after about six months of our meetings, and despite Diana's constant barrage of complaints that we were wasting time, there were enough hints to suggest that she actually wanted something from our relationship. This window—that she wanted something from our relationship—was important in helping me sustain my therapeutic efforts. Her rejection began to sound hollow and almost a like a litany we both had to endure at the beginning of every session before we could try to move on. Occasionally she spent the entire session crying and sobbing without explanation. After a few sessions where she just cried, she might than apologize for being such a "baby." In general she could not articulate why she was crying except to say, because "I am so worthless and pathetic . . . I'm a loser and I will always be a loser . . . I'm a piece of shit, garbage . . . You only see me because I am so pathetic . . ." Nevertheless, Diana rarely missed appointments and typically came to my waiting room early and sat and read magazines. My phone answering machine was filled with late night calls but with no messages recorded. I speculated that it was Diana calling to hear my voice. She denied this.

I arranged for a psychopharmacologistto meet with Diana, and she reluctantly agreed to try a variety of medications to relieve some of her depression. They appeared to have had little effect. It was necessary to hospitalize Diana multiple times, and she spent about a quarter of the four-and-a-half years we worked together in a locked psychiatric unit. Such hospitalization were indicated when Diana admitted to severe suicidal impulses or when she made a suicide attempt with an overdose of pills. Diana and I had over the many months made enough of a therapeutic alliance that she would voluntarily enter the hospital if I told her it was necessary. She also knew that I would involuntarily commit her to the hospital if she refused. At times she seemed relieved when I insisted that she enter the hospital. I told her "There are no alternatives and I would not negotiate for your life." When she was in the hospital she quickly alienated the staff. Her sullen, rejecting manner, her dismissal of anyone who tried to befriend her and her self-isolation manner set the stage for periods when she would then engage in serious head banging or self-mutilation with secreted sharp objects. As her therapist I had to spend a good deal of time working with the hospital staff to maintain their morale and willingness to continue to try to engage this young woman and not to succumb to her efforts to alienate everyone. During a number of these hospitalizations I was able to have several associates agree to see Diana in consultation since I too was feeling rather despairing in my attempts to treat her. Diana refused to talk with them and accused me of trying to "unload her."

During a three-month period in our third year of therapy, Diana came to my office daily but then refused to talk. She did not say a word but just sat with her head down. Sometimes during these sessions I tried to put into words what I thought was going on in her mind—her anger with me, her attempt to isolate herself and protect herself from her thoughts, and her efforts to drive me away. At other times we sat in silence. After leaving my office following these silent sessions she sent me daily letters—often several in one day (there were over one hundred letters in this three-month period), describing in exquisite detail her inner thoughts and feelings. The themes were generally how worthless she was, "Everyone knows that except maybe you . . . my mother knew that."

A sample of the quotes from her letters include, "I'm a piece of shit . . . People who try to be nice to me are either stupid or lying—like you . . . I'll start to depend on them and then they will shit all over me and get rid of me . . . So keep the fuck out of my life . . . You are wasting your time . . . You see me only because my old man pays you . . . Get a life." She felt hopeless and worthless. "I won't talk to you because I like you. Maybe I can trust you— but that always leads to me getting smashed and disappointed . . . OK you seem honest—but so what? . . . Where will that get me . . . My father was a pervert, and you're also probably a pervert . . . You probably also want to fuck me . . . I'm sorry I said that . . . You're probably a good person and I'm sorry I'm so rotten . . . You're leading me into a trap and I will be in hell and you will be laughing . . . Sooner or later I'm going to kill myself—like my stupid cow mother . . . I just can't stand how rotten I always feel . . . You don't know what it's like to feel horrible, empty, angry all the time . . . I can't stand it . . . Please stop seeing me—this is a waste of time and you make it worse . . . Thank you for putting up with me—I'm a bitch—how can you tolerate me . . . When will you give up . . . Everyone does—you'll see."

For reasons that were unclear, after three months of silence and over one hundred letters—Diana began to talk in our session. She could not explain her silences, except "maybe I was getting too close to you so I couldn't talk to you."

Diana rarely missed a session. Most of the time she spent telling me what a terrible person she was, and how empty she felt. I told her about how I understood the origins of this emptiness and fear of abandonment and that it made me angry and sad when I thought of how she was treated and "thrown away" as an infant. I knew that Diana was listening and she even acknowledged that what I said made sense but it did not take away her sad feelings and her sense of worthlessness.

In the early part of our fourth year of work Diana seemed to soften to me. She might ask me questions about practical matters like where to find an apartment. She enrolled in the local community college and though she associated with no one, she enjoyed the intellectual challenge and inquired about courses to take. On occasion she even said, "Thanks for putting up with me."

But then "the depression storm" blew in again and she became increasingly depressed and suicidal. It was not clear why this happened. Nothing had changed in her outside world, but she again began slicing up her forearms. She then missed a Monday appointment, and I had not seen her over the weekend. I called the police who were able to enter her apartment and found her on the floor in a coma. She was hospitalized but was left with a paralyzed left leg and left arm from the pressure on the nerves while she was unconscious. She remained in the hospital for two months to protect her from herself and for physical rehabilitation. She could ultimately get around using a crutch. Though I always kept Diana's father informed about his daughter's status—and about her paralysis— he never came to see her. When I spoke to him on the phone (about once a month) he said he was not well, he had a "bad heart" and could not tolerate seeing his daughter—it would "kill me." He said Diana reminded him of his wife who committed suicide.

Diana was ultimately discharged from the hospital but now because of her physical disability she needed an aid to be with her several hours a day to help her manage. We continued to meet daily and continued to struggle with her depression and self-loathing. She resumed some of her courses at the community college. She spoke with some optimism about her summer plans and then she failed to arrive for a Monday appointment, and she could not be found in her apartment. Several days later the police called. She was found in a local hotel and had committed suicide by an overdose of pills and alcohol.

Diana left a suicide note. The writing became increasingly scribbled and disorganized as she was sinking into a coma. She wrote, "Dr. Fischer, I must die. I always feel so terrible. None of the pills I took were yours . . . the ones that you ordered for me are still in my apartment . . . so many people will be happier and better off if I am dead . . . you were a good doctor . . . I was a bad patient . . . please don't be angry with me . . ."

Diana comments

This case was included in this book because it reflects on important aspects of the human condition—particularly the development of self-image and self-worth. Diana was haunted throughout her short life with an image of herself as a worthless and disposable piece of trash. How she thought, acted, and felt was infused with this self-perception. This depreciated self-worth colored the lenses through which she saw herself, the world and the people around her. This fundamental view of herself made it almost impossible for her to tolerate her being and to relate to people in a trusting or even neutral manner. From her earliest experiences, she knew "in her bones" that she was worthless and disposable and that all relationships were noxious and ultimately filled with pain. This is how she "knew" relationships to be. Expecting this and "knowing" the world in this way, she in fact became obnoxious, off-putting, angry, rejecting, and at times hateful. In essence she was molding or transforming the external world to confirm her internal reality that she was worthless and obnoxious. Those around her behaved accordingly. After a period of tolerating her, people rejected her. It was painful trying to relate to Diana. Acquaintances avoided and abandoned her and thereby fulfilled her self-perception and her view of the world. Diana thereby realized her expectations of being a disposable and hateful child and adult.

In reviewing Diana's early history one can easily see how this negative self-image evolved. While still in utero her mother tried to dispose of her. This pattern persisted throughout childhood with mother's rejection, anger, and desertions. There was no one to serve as a constant, reliable, and positive human in her life for attachment and sustenance. Nurses came and went, her father was unable to be emotionally available and even her older brother was off in his own sphere of drugs. Diana's world was tumultuous, rejecting, and filled with anger and often on the verge of outbreaks of violence between her parents. In her immature thinking she was the center and the cause of all this, and thus she was to blame for all this unhappiness and the rage that surrounded her. In her view, she was obviously the noxious and hateful one. Mother's suicide when Diana was eight years old confirmed Diana's "badness" and served to solidify her negative self-image. Her father's attention to her after his wife died was confusing to this prepubescent child, and it was not clear to her if he was attending to her needs or attempting to deal with his own loss.

It was on this background that efforts at psychotherapy unfolded. From Diana's perspective human contact was not to be trusted, it could only lead to abandonment, and hurt. She was attached to no one and attachment itself was to be defensively avoided. Yet she felt so alone, needy, empty, and chronically depressed. She reflexively had to bite the hand of anyone who tried to reach out to her. To use a medical analogy—Diana's disease had evolved from a deficiency problem to a malabsorption disease. Trying to provide her some of the things she missed as an infant—relationships of consistency, love, and positive feedback—were not in themselves helpful, because Diana at this point in her life could not "absorb" these elements of a relationship. She rejected positive human contact, because she experienced it as dangerous, false, and unpredictable. She was suspicious and angry with those who tried to be helpful (schoolmates, teachers, therapists). She was alone and starving in a sea of plenty. Diana saw suicide as the only way out of her intolerable dilemma and her chronic and painful despair.

Establishing a therapeutic or working alliance with Diana, given her view of the world, was extremely challenging. Diana's multiple therapists were experienced as intruders, enemies, and people who were intent on ultimately hurting her. As noted above Diana felt the need to transform her therapists to conform to her internal view of the world. She was rejecting, hostile, and her behavior was at times obnoxious. It is not surprising that she had seen three or four therapist before we met. My colleague who asked me to see her indicated that he felt "totally drained" by her. Though Electric Shock Therapy can be useful is some situations, I wondered if the EST that Diana received several years before we started working together, was an intervention that reflected some of the anger and rejection Diana was capable of generating in those with whom she came in contact. When Diana attacked and demeaned it required a great deal of "stepping back," understanding and self-reflection to avoid becoming punitive and being transformed into one of her "adversaries."

Having a patient with whom you have worked intensively over several years commit suicide is of course a jarring experience. Sadness, a sense of failure, self-questioning, self-doubt, and a sense of personal responsibility (should I have done something differently?) were certainly part my emotional response. It was an emotional response that can linger and be reawakened by writing this narrative.

8

Frankie—
The urge to be beaten-up

Frankie, age seven, was constantly being teased and beaten up at school. He often came home bruised, scratched, and with his eyeglasses broken. From teachers' reports and his own descriptions, it was clear that he provoked these attacks. He was physically awkward and used too many "big words," and became an easy target for abuse. Frankie said he had to be "honest" with his classmates so without invitation he would tell them that they were smelly or ugly or dumb, and he received the expected response—a punch in the nose. Though he was advised and scolded by parents not to be "so honest," he seemed unable to restrain himself, and indeed it appeared as if he received some gratification in being beaten up and teased. His parents noticed that Frankie often smiled and seemed "gleeful" when he described some of these encounters with classmate and how his glasses were again broken. Also the teachers commented that while he was being beaten up by his classmates, he would howl and cry for help; yet he looked disappointed and was resistant when a staff member came to his aid. Other than in these confrontations with classmates, the teachers saw Frankie as a shy, retiring youngster and someone who tended to remain silent and in the background. The faculty at his parochial school became alarmed when Frankie asked them several times if suicide was a sin. Questioned why he wanted to know, he just shrugged his shoulders and said, "I'm just curious."

Frankie was an only child. He wore large glasses—much too big for his small face, and he had a "bowl" haircut. His clothing always seemed inappropriate for a child his age. Indeed he looked "weird," as if he were out of touch with other kids. It was easy for me to see how he could become a target for bullying by other children.

Both parents were professionals. Mother was proficient, hard-driving and demanding in her work. She held a high position in her field and said she always felt very busy and pressured. She had had mixed feelings about having a child and indicated that she was "forced into it" by her husband. She worried that having a child would interfere with her professional activities, and two weeks after Frankie was born she returned to her full-time work. She said that since Frankie could not yet speak he would not notice or be upset by the separation. She also admitted that she was emotionally illequipped to be a mother since her own child-hood had been "rotten." Father, on the other hand, was very anxious to have a child though his reasons were not clear. Though professionally well trained, he barely survived at his job. His wife reported that his work was sloppy, often tardy, and dis-organized. Further, that he related poorly to clients and associates. Father indicated that dismissal from his job always seemed "around the corner," and even after many years he remained at an entry level in his firm. Like his son Frankie, he too looked "out of touch." He had a mop of hair, frizzled, and in disarray. The lenses of his eyeglasses were coke-bottle-thick, distorting his eyes. His clothing was mismatched and crumpled. He described feeling very close to his son and enjoyed playing games with him—especially "tag" and "war" games. He acknowledged that he was unable to set limits or discipline his son and readily described feeling more like a playmate to Frankie than an adult parent.

The parents said that they fought with each other constantly —, about money, chores around their home, and responsibilities and roles in raising Frankie. Mother accused father of being a poor role model and not being able to set limits or establish some discipline. Father accused mother of being harsh, insensitive, cold, and unavailable. On a number of occasions, neighbors called the police because of the loud and abusive yelling from their apartment, claiming it sounded as if someone was being murdered.

I met with Frankie four days a week and saw the parents together once a month. Our work continued for three-and-a-half years. The parents arranged their schedules so they could alternate bringing Frankie to my office and picking him up. Whereas mother was always on time dropping her son off and picking him up, father, in the beginning of our therapy, somehow got lost and was late in picking Frankie up from our sessions.

From the onset Frankie moved around my office and playroom with great energy and apparent ease. He was curious and he explored all available corners, the spaces under the furniture, and the desk drawers. He climbed under my couch, hid momentarily, and then jumped out in an effort to frighten me. He often quizzically sniffed at objects "just like my gerbils." He stared at my face as we played checkers, and talked, and wondered if a picture on my wall of Freud was a picture of me.

War games with toy soldiers and guns held his attention for many months. He built block castles to the highest level and then loudly smashed them to the ground. When we played cards—his favorite game was "war"—he became very animated and regularly cheated in order to win. On many occasions he arrived with scratches on his face and was often very excited, and somewhat agitated. He might jump up and down on my couch. At times I found it necessary to set boundaries as to what he could do and where he could explore in my office / playroom. He easily complied with my rules and then moved on to other activities. There was a certain pressure to his speech as he described his play, and he tended to speak in polysyllabic words—far beyond his agelevel. Despite his abounding energy and "grown-up" talk, I could sense that he was very sad and worried. He told me details about his gerbils; they were lonely, they had no friends and smelled bad. I asked him about his questions to teachers about suicide and he quickly said, "I was just teasing them. They looked so worried . . . They are really dumb."

As Frankie played out and thereby "told me" some of his worries and about his unhappiness, I, in running commentary, tried to put into words what I felt he was trying to tell me by his actions. "Frankie, I think you keep very, very, very busy in here to push away some of those sad feelings just like the gerbils." I also wondered out loud if getting into fights with classmates was better than being alone and forgotten. I told him I knew he liked to win at war card games and sometimes he had to make up his own rules so "you know how it will turn out. Sometimes you don't know how wars between mom and dad at home will work out." I thought out loud if his trying to scare me when he jumped out from underneath the couch was his way of telling me how he felt sometimes at home—"scared." I said I knew that sometimes he didn't like my "rules," but I wondered if "knowing what you can do in my office and some things you cannot do makes you feel more comfortable." My putting his worries into words was essential to our therapeutic work. By "symbolizing" his poorly articulated fears, worries, and fantasies, we were opening a new avenue for mastery of these sources of anxiety—avenues for expression and mastery other than action that was often disruptive and self-defeating. Frankie listened intensely to my running comments but rarely responded except in his play.

After we played a game involving a circus and clowns, he told me that he really enjoyed being the clown at school. "The punches don't bother me—but I don't like the pinches." He showed me a few bruises on his arms.

In the second year of our meetings, one particular activity occupied the sessions. With much pressure and excitement he opened one of my desk drawers (an area that was "in bounds" for him to use) and proceeded to completely cover the opening with multiple pieces of paper and Scotch Tape. This was to be the "landing field." He then made a paper airplane with a paper clip that was to be part of the landing gear. The paper clip was bent open so a pointed wire was protruding from the bottom of the plane. In an excited, loud voice he described, and played out how the airplane flew around and then landed on the airfield. The paper clip landing gear ripped into the paper landing field. After five or six such landings, the airfield was torn to shreds. Frankie would hurriedly remove the remnants and energetically construct a new landing field with paper and tape. With anxious glee and shouting, he repeated this play over and over again.

As I watched and commented on this pressured activity it became clear to me that Frankie was telling me about the sexual activities between his parents that he was exposed to and which excited him and worried him a lot. The yelling, shouts, piercing, ripping, apparent anger, and destruction were his understanding of what he was hearing from his parents' bedroom, and the imagined scenario was being enacted in my office, on my desk drawer, and perhaps on me. After wondering about this to myself, I began speculating out loud in running commentary as the airstrips were being constructed and ripped apart. "You must get very excited and worried when you hear the loud sounds from mommy and daddy's bedroom at night time. Maybe when you hear all that racket you wonder if someone is getting hurt or ripped—just like the airfields." Frankie ignored my comments. He continued to construct and destroy without pause—but I knew he heard me and heard me well.

Frankie was a very bright and creative child. Soon after I commented on his hearing the noises from his parents' bedroom, he brought in a large book that gave instructions on how to construct paper airplanes and how to make them fly in "just the right way." It was rather impressive with how skillful Frankie was in correctly folding the paper and then predicting accurately the flight pattern of his missile. I noted how important it was to him to have such control of his airplanes, since the life around him— at school and especially at home—was so out of control. Following such comments, predictably many of the airplanes ended up hitting me. Frankie was unhappy and upset about my comments and loudly said, "Just play and don't talk." Frankie wanted me to be his playmate like his Father—without direction or boundaries.

My monthly meetings with the parents were informative and important therapeutically. Both mother and father had had difficult childhoods. Mother's parents were high achieving, harsh, and demanding. Academic achievement was rewarded but little else. Affection and tenderness were minimal and conditional. The maternal grandfather was a revered scholar who terrified his students and his family. Mother grew up always feeling inadequate and certainly not equipped to raise a child. She retreated into her all-absorbing career. Father's childhood was characterized as impoverished and unhappy. Economic woes prevailed at home and his parents constantly complained of being oppressed by "the system." As a youngster, father had few friends, rarely played with others, and grew up feeling that he had missed having a childhood. He often went to school wearing tattered and unclean clothing and was treated like an outsider. Father acknowledged that he very much loved being Frankie's playmate —, playing games, teasing and "horsing around."

In my sessions with the parents I was quite direct. For instance, very early on I told the parents that being late to pick up their son was totally unacceptable. My office was in a large hospital setting with a communal waiting area, and Frankie was frightened when he was left waiting and unsure if someone was going to pick him up. After getting some better sense of the parents, I strongly recommended that both parents get into individual therapy to help them deal with their inner conflicts and some of their struggles with each other. Mother readily complied and entered individual treatment. Father refused. Around the time that Frankie was preoccupied and pressured in our sessions with his airplane / landing field "play," I asked the parents about their sexual life together. They reported that despite other marital difficulties, sex was mutually very enjoyable, frequent, and passionate. When I raised the issue of Frankie's exposure to this activity—they indicated that they doubted if Frankie could either witness or hear their nighttime activities. They did acknowledge, however, that Frankie was a very curious youngster, that he could hide in the strangest places, and their apartment was rather small. I told them that I was rather certain that Frankie did hear noises from their bedroom and that it was likely that he was overly excited and frightened by the noises and by his vivid imagination. I told the parents that they should be more discreet, and set firmer limits on what Frankie might be exposed to.

In a more general way, I told the parents that despite their own personal difficulties, it was important to Frankie that they behave like parents—not playmates or absentee caretakers. Frankie was a child, and he needed safe and reliable adult parents. Though my comments and approach were somewhat harsh and direct—I thought they were important for Frankie's growth. The parents indicated that they were willing to comply with my instructions and to try to modify their behavior—in large part because Frankie was improving since he started therapy. He was making a far better adjustment at school and developing some neighborhood friends. The parents acknowledged and appreciated these changes but also expressed their concern that Frankie would become too attached to me and they would "lose" their son.

Frankie did very well in his therapy and after three-and-a-half years we decided to stop and "see how it goes." In addition to relating much better to peers and having several good friends, he was far less worried, preoccupied and drained by his internal conflicts. He no longer seemed depressed and lonely. He was excelling in his schoolwork, seemed to be liked by his teachers, and was playing soccer after school.

Several years after Frankie finished his analysis, he called me and asked for an appointment. Upon seeing him I was impressed by a very handsome looking young adult who spoke with confidence and charm. He was now a university student and wanted to meet with me a few times to talk about career choices. He was seriously considering going to medical school and maybe becoming a psychiatrist, "maybe even a psychoanalyst." He lived on the university campus and described an active and rich social life. He occasionally visited his parents and sadly told me that they had not changed much. His mother still was totally absorbed in her career and did little else, and his father seemed depressed and often "lost." His father still bemoaned the fact that Frankie had decided to move away from home when he entered college.

Frankie and I met a few times and then we said "good-bye."

Frankie comments

Frankie was overcome with feelings of sadness, loneliness, anger, and confusion. He had no words for his worries. He could only obtain relief through action—and his actions often caused him considerable grief. Deliberation and conflict resolution requires awareness of thoughts and feelings, and then the words with which to identify them. Action yielded temporary relief for his pent up feelings toward his classmates. ,The result however was that he was left isolated and even more hurt, angry, sad and fearful. He had no way out of this escalating and debilitating cycle.

In his frantic play in my office, Frankie conveyed a wide array of his inner worries, his anger, fears, and confusion. He was anxious and agitated—so he jumped on my couch until I had to set boundaries for him. The life around him—at home and at school—felt out of control—so he tried to control me and how our card games turned out. He was frightened by the unpredictable fights at home so he jumped out from under the couch to frighten me and tell me in action how he felt when unexpected things happened to him. When Frankie did not like what I said he skillfully made airplanes to strike me. His exposure at home to his parents' sexual activity was confusing, sounded murderous, and was overly stimulating. With great gusto and vividness he acted this out in the airplane landing scenarios where the strip was brutally ripped apart. His "play" was pressured and on the verge of being out-of-control.

So we worked on putting names to feelings—feelings that were leading to selfdestructive actions—actions that were resulting in just what it was he was trying to avoid—more hurt, anger, and sadness and a sense of helplessness. Words and meanings were supplied by my running commentary and verbal interventions. Clarifications and explanations were important building blocks in Frankie's developing the ability to think about his overwhelming, confusing, and mysterious inner world. My comments also conveyed my understanding that he had an inner world of feelings and thoughts and that this was driving his impulsive action. Frankie slowly became aware of and curious about what was happening inside his head.

At first he was not able to connect his unhappy lonesome feelings with his pressure to be "honest" with schoolmates and then getting beaten up. Nor could he connect his jumping up and down on my couch with his worry that his father might not pick him up or that he could not sleep at night because he was afraid his mother was being killed in the next room.

Frankie had always been interested in how things worked. In psychotherapy he turned curiosity inward and began to name and acknowledge feelings and worries. He started to figure out the puzzle of how this led to impulsive and hurtful actions with such dire results.

Working with children has at least two advantages in terms of outcome. One is that there is greater plasticity in a youngster's personality and change is therefore far more achievable. And second is that the developmental thrust of childhood propels and facilitates therapeutic change. Frankie gradually began to be in greater control of his actions. He was increasingly aware of his feelings and impulses and they no longer ran his life. He was more in control of his inner conflicts and this gave him far more room to grow.

Finally, it was easy to see how unresolved struggles and dysfunction is transmitted from one generation to the next. Both Frankie's parents had very difficult childhood experiences. It was clear that Frankie was on his way to incorporating and repeating their difficulties. His intense psychotherapy allowed him to find a different path.

9

Annie—
Starving to death to keep in control

hen I first met Annie in consultation I was horrified. She appeared as if she had just emerged from a Nazi concentration camp. She was sixteen years old and had the appearance of a fragile porcelain figurine draped in large bulky clothing. She looked physically ill, weighed perhaps seventy pounds, and her complexion was sallow. She looked like a prepubescent unhealthy eleven-year-old child with large eyes too big for her emaciated face. She was articulate, seemed intelligent and despite her cachectic appearance, had an engaging manner. She came to see me because her parents insisted.

Annie dated her difficulties to six months prior to our consultation when she found herself becoming increasingly depressed and feeling less and less interested in schoolwork. She realized that she was withdrawing from her friends and was lacking in enthusiasm for all her activities. Initially she assumed she needed a new stimulating interest, but her feelings of apathy were persistent. She was not aware of any precipitating factors in her worsening depression, but characteristically accepted her parents' pressure to seek psychiatric consultation. As an aside she reported that she had lost a lot of weight but this was not a "big deal," and she was not sure why her family doctor made such a fuss about it. It also was not a "big deal" that her menstrual periods had stopped for no apparent reason.

Annie's parents dated her difficulties further back to at least one year prior to the consultation when their daughter starting dieting. The reason given for the diet was that Annie was about five pounds overweight. At the time, Annie was also involved in a vigorous swimming program at school. Over the next year, Annie lost approximately thirty pounds and her menstrual periods had stopped. The parents and the family physician were alarmed about the youngster's physical health but despite their warnings and threats, Annie persisted in her diet. Annie was not overtly concerned about her weight loss that soon became quite visible, nor did she express concern about her amenorrhea. The family physician could find nothing wrong physically with Annie other than her weight loss. The parents were not initially aware of any signs of depression but added that their daughter's characteristic indecisiveness might have blended into and disguised any depressive features.

Annie was a much-desired firstborn child. Pregnancy and delivery were described as normal and "easy." Reportedly Annie was very colicky and mother was told that her daughter was allergic to milk and breast-feeding was discontinued after several weeks. The family pediatrician treated the colic by having the parents give Annie enemas almost daily for the first three months. Weight gain was normal, and she was weaned from the bottle when she was two-and-a-half-years old. Bowel and bladder training were "natural" and diapers were not needed by age three. Annie was speaking well at age two, and in general the parents saw their daughter as a bright, lively, and precocious youngster.

At the age of two it was discovered that Annie had some ure-thral constriction and was cystoscoped several times. She was then hospitalized for a number of days and was repeatedly cath-eterized. Though mother stayed with Annie throughout the hospitalization, Annie seemed very distressed and mother recalled thinking at the time that someday the trauma of these procedures would cause her daughter problems.

In addition, from the age of one to three, Annie had four or five ear infections. The pediatrician reportedly did not believe in antibi-otic therapy, and on each occasion he had Annie held down and he incised her eardrum. The parents were uneasy about their pediatri-cian's treatment of the colic, the ear infections, and the bladder dif-ficulties, but he was a very prominent and highly respected member of the medical community, and it was only after Annie's third year that they felt confident enough to change doctors.

Annie had a favorite blanket that she carried around until she was three-and-a-half. There were no major separations from parents until Annie was thirteen. She entered nursery school at three, and the separation did not appear particularly distressing. From school reports, Annie's adjustment to school went quite smoothly. At three-and-a-half a sibling was born. There was some early show of resentment and some resistance to going to school but this was transient. Routine school psychological testing showed her to be somewhat uneasy about expressing angry feelings for fear that her dependency needs would be denied. Teachers noted that Annie could be quite stubborn and inflexible but in general she was described as a very bright, very sociable, and delightful youngster.

In describing their daughter's personality in the recent years, the parents noted that Annie tended to be rather indecisive and would agonize over every decision. She was also called "nonag-gressive" and had difficulties in initiating activities and was reluctant to approach peers to make friends. Once a friendship was initiated however, she usually was very well liked. In a related fashion she had to be coaxed and pushed into new experiences such as going on trips or joining a new group. Once she was launched in a new activity, however, she became very involved and then might become self-critical because of the time she had wasted in getting started. Father noted that Annie tended to "give you what you want." She rarely rebelled and came across as "an ideal child with no major problems." There was never a discipline problem, and she appeared to enjoy rather open and warm relationships with both parents. She was consistently on the school honor roll and tended to be a serious and hard working student. The parents noted, however, that if Annie did not understand a book or subject totally, she would often throw up her hands in disgust and in despair and say, "I can't figure this whole thing out."

Annie was well prepared for menarche by her mother which was at about age thirteen. Her periods were regular and not associated with any appreciable discomfort. She did not appear particularly upset when her menstrual periods stopped one year prior to coming for psychiatric consultation.

Initially I met with the parents together and then interviewed them separately, primarily for history taking. Over the next five years there were two or three brief meetings with me and perhaps a half dozen phone calls. Briefly both parents were professionals in their midforties and both came across as warm, articulate, intelligent, and sensitive people who were deeply concerned about their daughter and dedicated to supporting her treatment. Though both were quite active in community life, they spent a great deal of time with their children and seemed genuinely warm, concerned, and responsive. My impression of the parents was quite positive and this was generally confirmed by Annie's description of them throughout the analysis. Her main complaints about her parents ranged from their being too worried about her eating habits and an annoying quality of indecisiveness and uncertainly on mother's part. There was no family history of emotional difficulty and parents reportedly related well to each other.

In describing Annie's treatment, daily sessions over a five-year period, I will focus primarily on the first two-and-a-half years of our work together since this was a period of great turmoil and struggle in the therapeutic encounter. The analysis was conducted face-to-face and Annie was almost always on time, rarely missed appointments and there were no major interruptions other than planned summer vacations.

From the earliest weeks of this analysis there was an intense and painful engagement. Soon after the initial evaluative interviews, Annie presented herself as a helpless, whining, angry, little girl. Though sixteen years old, her emaciated pale appearance, her ill fitting baggy clothing, and her plaintive manner gave her the appearance of a ten- or eleven-year-old petulant, injured, and prepubescent child. There was a steady stream of anguished complaints and requests for help. "I don't know what to say." "Nothing is on my mind." "What should I talk about?" "My thoughts fly by and they don't mean anything." "Why don't you ask me questions or tell me what to talk about?" Her pleas for help had an edge of demanding indictment and were interspersed with long silences during which time Annie seemed uncomfortable, irritable, and agitated. She thrashed around in her chair. If she brought up an event that occurred at school, a thought, a worry—her descriptions and elaborations were meager and her associations minimal. Efforts to draw her out regarding details of her current life events, school, home, friends, her feelings and thoughts in the analytic sessions, were summarily dismissed as unimportant. She seemed annoyed, impatient, and angry at my inquiries or observations.

There was a great deal of self-depreciation and self-punitive preoccupation. She was critical of most things she did—her passivity, her paralyzing indecisiveness—and indicated that failure pervaded all sectors of her life. Her self-directed rage was accompanied by anguished crying and occasionally she punched her leg in disgust as she talked. Every decision, what dress to wear or what school courses to take, was a major struggle with overt and covert efforts to draw me into the fray. "I need advice, not analysis," she shrieked. "I need help, tell me what to do," she demanded as tears rolled down her face. Desperate efforts at self-control were prominent in her daily life with weight control being central. Annie's specific weight was rarely mentioned. Prior to beginning the analysis I decided that Annie would continue to see her internist on a regular basis and that he would call me if a medical emergency was at hand. Annie described a very rigid self-imposed diet with carefully calculated caloric intake. Minor deviations from her self-prescribed diet stimulated much self-depreciation and remorse. There were occasional "eating binges" ranging from truly excessive intake to minor infractions such as having an extra graham cracker, and this was followed by Annie's tearful description of her self-disgust and feeling "crazy" and "out-of-control." Indeed, after one such infraction of her "rules" she experienced the feeling that her body was "disintegrating" and that she was "coming apart." Surrounding her long silences there emerged from the analytic material a related issue about her fear of talking too freely with me. Her concern was that if she let herself talk about all the things on her mind, all her worries and her thoughts, she might not be able to stop, would lose control and terrible and embarrassing things might flow out.

During this early phase of the analysis there was a steady

request that I structure the sessions by asking questions, making suggestions of topics or by answering various queries. Annie pleaded, demanded, and put pressure on me to intervene. This was parallel to the many anecdotes about the flood of requests directed toward her parents, especially her father, to help organize her life. Reportedly, if father did succumb to her demands, for instance to select her school schedule, she became more uncertain and then felt totally helpless, paralyzed by indecision, and filled with self-hatred for being such a "wimp." My efforts to engage Annie in looking at this pattern, to draw her out about her need for such guidance and intervention and to clarify and better understand these steady demands, were met by Annie's tearful and angry protests. She expressed total frustration with whatever I did or did not say. If I made a clarifying or interpretive comment, I was summarily dismissed and disdainfully told, "It isn't important. I don't agree, forget it." If I was quiet and pensive, Annie raged on how she was not being helped and in fact she felt I was tormenting her. On a number of occasions if Annie left a session particularly distraught, she subsequently described feeling "disorganized" and a sense that somehow her body was "disintegrating."

Though Annie's behavior in the analysis was vivid and her affect intense, the actual content of what she said was repetitive, impoverished, and generally vague. She did not report dreams or fantasies and was most reluctant to elaborate or associate to the thoughts and feelings that she was having. With great frustration she complained that she could not put her thoughts into words, and a nebulous vague quality prevailed. She could report on some of her daily life events, but this inevitably led to the tearful litany of how inadequate and disgusting she was and how paralyzed she was in making the most simple decisions.

The ensuing pleas and demands for help, the veiled threats,

crying and screaming were not experience by me as shallow manipulations or hollow histrionics. Annie was in considerable distress and efforts to clarify and understand this distress led to further anguished crying and / or disdainful dismissal.

A specific example may be helpful in conveying the clinical picture: In the beginning of the second year in analysis, Annie arrived at my office looking unusually sullen and disheveled. She then asked about the parking area outside my office and asked where she might park her car. This was an unusual question since Annie had been driving to my office for many months, the parking spaces were well demarcated and when we started the analysis, I had clearly indicated the areas available for parking. I asked about her query—since she had been using the lot for many months. Annie became tearful, annoyed, and complained, "just tell me—I'm not sure—it's confusing." As I gently tried to draw her out about her confusion and wondered about her feeling so tearful and annoyed, Annie became more agitated and angry and shouted, "Please just tell me—you must know—why don't you just tell me? Why must you analyze everything?" Efforts on my part to note and try to understand the situation, to comment on her pressure for me to give her further direction and provide her with more structure and guidelines, were met with either periods of sullen silence, tearful outbursts of anger, and accusations that I was tormenting her and then loud sobbing. This lasted for most of the session. Among other things, I was now feeling rather uncomfortable about this sobbing and apparently distraught youngster leaving my office and driving through the city to school. I therefore suggested to her that it might be a good idea for her to use my waiting room, which was off to the side, for a few minutes before leaving the building. My suggestion was met by silence.

After Annie left and I was with my next patient, I was aware of uneasiness and a nagging preoccupation. I did not know if Annie had heeded my suggestion. I had the thought of calling her school to find out if she had arrived—but I then elected not to act on this inclination. The next day Annie immediately started the session by railing at me for telling her what to do in the previous session and vigorously told me that she had not stayed in the waiting room and resented my treating her like a "baby" or a "psycho." She went on to describe how she did not like it when people told her what to do—that she did not like feeling like a patient, and furthermore, did not know why she was seeing me in the first place.

The impact of this almost daily assault on me was not insignificant—a euphemistic way of saying I felt frazzled, frustrated, abused, despairing, drained, and initially bewildered by this intense and seemingly chaotic engagement. At times I felt an inner pressure to somehow be soothing, give direction or provide greater structure. At times I began to have serious doubts about my initial assessment of Annie and wondered if indeed a more structured, supportive mode of therapy was indicated. For the first two to three years Annie continued to look physically quite ill and fragile and there was the temptation to hospitalize her or to provide greater structure and direction. I knew, however, that such an approach would not be helpful in the long-term and indeed would be counterproductive.

In the third year of our work, gradual but important shifts became evident. Annie continued to rage and rail at me for things I said or things I failed to say—but it was noticeable that she was "stepping back" and thinking about what was unfolding between us and about the conflicts and struggles that we repeatedly witnessed, clarified, and underscored. Though the patterns of the first two years with the intense emotional outpouring were present, Annie could on occasion say, "OK, OK I know

what you're thinking but so what? What good does it do me?"
Or as tears rolled down her cheeks she might utter, "I can't stop
what I'm doing—I'm stuck and you are not helping much."
Though such comments carried mixed feelings and an ongoing
indictment, they also reflected Annie's increasing ability to
appreciate the drama that was being enacted between us. This
noticeable shift in her ability to be self-observant was also seen
in her applying some of the issues we talked about to relationships outside the analytic sphere. For instance, she wondered if
some of the friction she experienced with friends at school
when they tried to help her was because their offers made her
feel dumb and angry. She then blindly lashed out at these classmates. It was with considerable reluctance that Annie noticed
these gradual shifts in our relationship and in her contacts at
school. When we tried to understand her reluctance to acknowledge these small changes, it became clear that even the process
of "taking in" some of my comments and then agreeing that
they might be partially correct, represented an intrusion which
she reflexively had to reject.

By this time in our work, Annie was facing the prospect of
applying to colleges and of course wanted me to help her decide
if she should go away to college and thereby stop her therapy or
attend a local college and be able to continue our work. Annie
had outstanding SAT scores and a superb high school record and
she made it abundantly clear that she would be accepted to the
best schools in the country . . . but then there was the "analysis
thing." Annie knew I would not tell her what to do but she presented her dilemma in a teasing and semi-humorous manner.
Annie, by this time, was deeply invested in our work and she
knew it was important to continue.

At the end of about the third year of the analysis, I scribbled
in my daily notes that for the first time since we had been

working together, I noticed that Annie was a rather attractive teenager or perhaps more accurately young adult. She no longer looked prepubertal and indeed she had breasts. A week after this notation to myself, Annie casually mentioned that her menses had recently resumed after four years of her amenorrhea. Annie felt compelled to emphasize—"It's not a big deal."

Annie was dramatically improved in the fourth year of our work. She was a freshman at a local college and continued to remind me about all the wonderful schools she could have attended in distant states. She lived in the college dormitory with several new friends and reported having an active social life. She was of normal weight and her menses had resumed. She was a very attractive young woman. She was careful about eating only healthy foods. I continued to meet with her four times a week.

The atmosphere in my office had gradually but steadily changed. Whereas in the first two to three years of our work together, the shouting, crying, raging on and on were deafening and the content of what she actually said was repetitive and impoverished, in the last year-and-a -half of our work together, the richness of her thinking and her inner life became evident and was the focus of our sessions. She spoke of her terror of losing control and somehow losing herself and losing her identity. Taking long hot showers was important to her. While showering she could control the water pressure hitting her body and that gave her great comfort and "definition." She had uncertainties about dating and she wondered if the boys who were now regularly asking her out were really interested in her or just interested in her body. She reported dreams and was thoughtful in trying to understand what they meant. She talked of her future plans.

I had the pleasure of seeing Annie once or twice a year for several years after therapy ended. She was attending graduate school in another state and would call my office and tell me she was passing through town to see her parents, and if I had time she would like to stop in to say "hello." Her life was going well. She looked healthy and had an engaging and enjoyable social life. She was active at school and had assumed a leadership position. She was thinking about career options and politics and working as a negotiator were high on her list.

Annie comments

Working with Annie represented a therapeutic challenge—a challenge that could only be addressed if the underlying struggles that were driving her to self-destruction and an interpersonal pattern of engaging and then rejecting the people whom she needed most could be appreciated. The seemingly chaotic and painful dance that she was enacting in her daily life was clearly a reflection of the tumult and conflict of her inner world.

In the early months of the therapeutic encounter, it was tempting to get caught-up and lost in the intense drama that was unfolding. Annie's self-starvation, her emaciated ill appearance, her constant demands and then bitter rejection were provocative. It took several months of listening carefully, thinking, self-reflection, and being abused, for me to come to understand what this desperately ill young girl was experiencing and playing out in out therapy sessions. Annie could not tell me about her inner struggles because in large part she did not have the awareness or the words to articulate what was in her mind and what it was that was propelling her to self-abuse. She did not know how to understand her chaotic relationship with me—a relationship that she felt driven to enact.

As I came to understand it, Annie had been traumatized by the many body intrusions when she was an infant. The many intrusive procedures (enemas, myringotomies, cystoscopies, urethral dilatations) had compromised her normal developmental movement toward defining her own body and its boundaries, as well as experiencing and establishing her own body controls. All this was happening during the normal phase of childhood that developmental researchers and clinicians call the "rapprochement phase of the separation-individuation process"—a phase that generally occurs between eighteen and twenty-four months of age. During this important phase the infant is struggling to find a balance between her newly emerging autonomy and yet a continued need and yearning for attachment and dependence. There is an up and back, push–pull struggle. The toddler runs away with new skills in great joy and then looks back to be sure she is being followed and not alone and helpless in the newly discovered world. This normal dance of childhood (contributing to the "terrible twos") plays out as, "I am big and grown—don't help me but you MUST help me—I am helpless—you make me helpless." This phase is normally negotiated and the push–pull struggle resolved as the child matures and becomes more able to be autonomous and to individuate.

This important developmental rapprochement dance can reemerge with the onslaught of adolescent challenges when the demand for independence and rebellion are often coupled with behaviors that call forth and necessitate parental involvement.

In Annie's situation it seemed that the many body intrusions and traumata derailed the successful resolution of this important normal rapprochement struggle. As a young child this inner push–pull conflict could be partially submerged, but puberty put new demands on her body and her psyche. Her self-starvation proclaimed her autonomy and control of her own body—but in a way that necessitated that those around her intrude and intervene. In the waiting room example noted above, she looked as if she was outof-control and my suggestion that she sit in the waiting room for a few minutes was experienced as a painful intrusion and my taking control of her. She bitterly objected—"I am not a baby."

In our intense analytic relationship this dance was reawakened and became very much alive in our day-to-day sessions. I was also caught up in this enactment. I was pulled into the struggle by her utter despair and then immediately discarded and rejected by her rage and demand for autonomy. Her anguish and inner chaotic word became my chaotic world of trying to understand and to work with her. At times it felt like a lifeand-death struggle—for both of us. The struggle was enacted, clarified, talked about, and repeated again and again and again. It became apparent how this pressured push–pull struggle was ruling her life and formed the underlying dynamic driving her to starve herself. This reawakening and reenactment in the analytic space and our ongoing intense rapprochement struggle was central in our therapeutic progress and dominated the first two years of our analytic work. The internal struggle first had to be lived out and engaged in vivo with me, and then clarified, interpreted, and understood before her maddening dance could be resolved and put to rest.

Though Annie and I spoke often about the body intrusions in infancy and how controls were "taken" from her, of course she could not remember such early life events. Yet these events and patterns were indelible and "unforgettable." These intrusions and the impediment to developmental processes and individuation left their mark on her evolving personality structure. This developmental impediment set the stage for her lifeendangering struggle when puberty unbalanced her tenuous adjustment. Though she could not remember these early events, it was helpful to talk about them and to reconstruct what had happened and how they had affected her. In this way we were creating a coherent life narrative and this helped her understand and put in some meaningful order the chaos that had become her life in the past several years.

From my perspective this therapeutic engagement was also quite painful and stimulated a great deal of anxiety. I observed in my personal daily records that I scheduled extra time after each session with Annie to write my treatment notes and to have a soothing cup of tea. A significant number of people with anorexia nervosa die from selfstarvation and Annie looked emaciated and ill throughout this first half of our work. Having her internist see her regularly was helpful, however, she often came to my office looking as if she was on the verge of collapse.

Psychotherapeutic intervention is often abandoned in treating patients like Annie. The Sturm und Drang of the first few years of treatment often results in abandoning "talk therapy." Her vehement rejection of the therapist, the chaotic push–pull enactment, the anguish, and the reality of a medical crisis may make the psychological treatment seem impossible and imprudent. The therapist may feel the need to intervene by a variety of other modalities, such as hospitalization, forced feeding, confinement, medication, and some behavioral modification program. I have seen many such cases in consultation where this was the course of events and though sometimes the cycle of the eating disorder is forced to the background, I have been impressed that the individual is often left compromised in the growth and development of their personality potentials. In these situations the "cure" of the eating disorder is very costly.

SUMMARY AND DISCUSSION

The human condition and man's humanity are underscored in these nine vignettes. The clinical examples may at first appear extreme and alien, however on looking beneath the surface of the symptoms and maladaptive behavior, we can appreciate the struggles that are very much a part of being human. With "introspection, immersion, sensitivity, and a bit of courage," the reader can identify with the conflicts faced by each of these individuals. The resolutions they arrived at were temporarily useful but ultimately painful, self-destructive, and caused them considerable grief. These people are our friends, neighbors, our accountants, schoolteachers, and pupils—indeed "THEY ARE US." We recognize ourselves and our shared humanity in their unique struggles.

We know about others by knowing about ourselves. Personal experience and empathic attunement provide pathways for our appreciating the sadness, anxiety, and despair in others. We understand that the vicissitude of life and "rough spots" in living can foster anxiety, emotional withdrawal, and denial. The pressure to revisit past experiences—pleasurable and painful—can strongly color our daydreams and stir the scenarios encountered in our sleep. Our efforts to master and more fully digest hurts passively experienced can result in the active and repetitious reworking of the insult in the present. At times we seek heroes and superstars whom we idealize in an effort to magically bolster our own self-worth. In recollecting our past, we are prone to rewrite our histories and life narratives in keeping with our wishes and our disappointments.

Transference phenomena are ubiquitous, and they are part of how we relate to the people around us. We perceive and understand the surroundings through the lenses of our past experience and the dynamics of our inner worlds. Our reality is always personal and idiosyncratic. Occupying different vantage points, an inevitable gap exists between how we perceive ourselves and how we believe others experience us. At times this difference can be mystifying, disturbing, and result in a sense of having created a false self—a pretend façade—and then being burdened by the insecurity and fear of discovery and crushing humiliation.

Viewed on a spectrum, the line separating "normality" and dysfunction is narrow and distinctions are often arbitrary and difficult to determine. Most of the patients I have described were in many aspects of their lives "high functioning," and their inner disquiet was not apparent. They worked, had families, and they were involved creatively with the community. Dawn working as a valued senior executive was tormented by her inner and outer "blackness" and was burdened by identity confusion. Mary an articulate and successful graduate student was preoccupied with despair about her life and sought refuge in a series of wish-ful-filling delusions. Henry, a successful and productive professional, was aware of an inner emptiness and felt he was "sleepwalking" through life. Though Joan was a respectable and effective educator, she was privately enacting a life-threatening scenario of repeated pregnancies and dangerous abortions. Frankie, a willing victim was regularly bullied. Often such bullying is dealt with by neglect, assuming "boys will be boys" or hoping that the bully and the "easy mark" will "grow out of it." Such neglect would have seriously undermined Frankie's potential to be a creative and healthy adult.

The reasons that these individuals came to treatment were varied. Frankie, Diana, Claude, and Annie, though all distressed and seriously symptomatic, were brought to therapy by their parents. Without this outside intervention, it is unlikely that they would have been able to seek help by themselves. Henry was painfully aware that he was missing the joy and vitality of life. It was this awareness and unhappiness that motivated him to pursue treatment. Mary quickly turned treatment into a delusional effort to remedy her sadness and sooth her sense of failure in life. Dawn was having panic attacks; she was in acute distress and knew she needed help immediately. Joan sought treatment, as she was deeply depressed and racked with guilt.

It is important to note, that though both Dawn and Joan came to treatment with acute symptoms, it soon became clear that in both cases, beneath their presenting difficulties they were harboring lifelong struggles that were compromising their lives. Dawn was conflicted about her internal and external "blackness" and her identity confusion. Joan sat on a volcano of rage related to her intrusive, controlling father and colluding mother. The cycle of pregnancies and abortions that consumed Joan's life reflected the inner demons and ghosts she harbored since childhood. For both of these women, it might have been possible to treat their acute symptoms with medications alone—antidepressants and / or tranquilizers—and primarily attempt to alleviated the acute difficulties. This may have proven expedient, but such limited goals for these individuals would have been shortsighted and an unfortunate course to take. The acute symptoms were the "tip of the iceberg." They were a "call for help." It was the deeper and more chronic difficulties that burdened and drained their energies. It was these underlying struggles that had to be addressed and resolved for treatment to be meaningful and for their lives to become more fulfilling.

In reviewing these nine narratives, a central question emerges concerning etiology. Why was it that these conflicts and this inner turmoil resulted in serious dysfunction to these particular individuals? There are many people who have experienced childhood traumata, serious infantile illnesses, chronic distortions in their formative relationships, absent or inadequate parenting—and yet they seem not to suffer the same level of symptoms as the nine patients whom I have described. A complementary observation is that there are children and adults who have grown up in nurturing and healthy environments, but then as adults develop serious emotional disorders and are unable to cope with the vicissitudes of living.

Efforts to address such etiologic queries are many but the conclusions are often speculative and unsatisfying. In the narratives of my nine patients, I have underscored environmental agents contributing to the roots of their dysfunction. Included are such factors as trauma (Annie, Henry) and distorted and pathological interpersonal relationships (Joan, Diana, Frankie). Very little is known about the influence of biological and genetic endowments that might have made these individuals more vulnerable to emotional dysfunction. Also to be included in the etiological equation are fortuitous events and pure chance. If Henry's father had not suffered a massive heart attack while in bed with his son, or if Annie did not have urinary problems or had been treated by a more benign pediatrician—the outcomes of their adult difficulties may have been quite different. The interplay of these factors—environment, genes, hormones, and fortuitous life events, and other variables unknown to us, leads to a complexity that is at times mystifying and humbling in our efforts to understand the human condition.

Tracing adult dysfunction back to earlier etiological factors (a retrospective view), as I have done in the nine case histories, reconstructs a life narrative and serves to enhance our understanding of developmental processes. However, efforts to predict the future from early life events (a prospective view) are often far more difficult and speculative. The multiple variables, their unique interplay and the unanticipated events that impact on the individual as life unfolds—complicate and undermine such prognostic scenarios. Except in the most extreme situations, our predictive abilities are clouded with uncertainties and complexities.

In the nine cases I have outlined, the goals in therapy included understanding and resolving underlying conflicts, reducing symptoms and dysfunctional behaviors, and altering life trajectories to be more adaptive, more flexible, and more gratifying.

To realize these therapeutic goals, it was my judgment that insight-oriented, psychoanalytically informed treatment was indicated. In an attempt to demystify and shed light on this intensive process, examples of ongoing dialogue and fragments of the unfolding material have been outlined. Descriptive words, however, capture only a portion of the actual transaction that occurs between two people working together. The subtleties and complexities of such an interpersonal interaction are many. The verbal content is colored by and may even be contradicted by the silences, tones, gestures, and a myriad of unrecognized nonverbal cues. Two people meet frequently on a regular basis for a long period of time. Their roles can overlap and their therapeutic goals and expectations may differ. In the dyadic relationship, each person comes with his own personality and an unspoken world of memories, experiences, and dynamics. The patient seeks help because he is hurting, but yet he also tries to avoid hurtful thoughts and feelings. He wants to reveal secrets that are hidden—but such secrets are often not disclosed even to himself. The patient tries to speak freely to the helper, but the helper may simultaneously be experienced as a dangerous intruder in a private landscape. The therapist's comments may be accurate and helpful but at the same time his words may feel hurtful. The therapist as a participant-observer listens carefully to the words, the music, to the silences, and he tries to discern the foreground themes in the narrative, and what is implied and disguised in the background. The therapist must listen to himself—to the feelings, fantasies, and hypotheses that are evoked by the patient, and he must be attentive to how his comments, observations, and silences affect the other. He tries to experience and understand the I–Thou relationship and to clarify with the patient what is unfolding between them.

In this complex treatment relationship, several background elements are basic in establishing the frame for therapeutic engagement. The patient must feel safe, respected, and understood, and that the therapist is trustworthy, sensitive, and nonjudgmental. Such characteristics of the "background" may in themselves be helpful and emotionally supportive.

In this treatment setting, and in the foreground, there are two components of the helping process that are fundamental to therapeutic change: (1) The patient gains greater self-understanding, and (2) The patient experiences a new and growthful interpersonal relationship and perspective.

The importance of "knowing thyself," of attaining greater insight or self-understanding, was known to the ancient Greeks and was a concept that Sigmund Freud elaborated on in his assertion that intrinsic to psychoanalytic treatment was making that which is unconscious conscious. This increased self-awareness is therapeutic in helping to gain greater mastery and resolution of the unconscious intra-psychic conflicts and forces that are being expressed in symptom formation, feelings, and behavior.

In the nine cases presented, it was clear that the individuals though seriously burdened with psychic pain and self-destructive behaviors, were unaware of the underlying source of their dysfunction. Henry knew that he was not fully in touch with the world around him, but he was mystified as to why he seemed to be "sleepwalking" through life. Joan hated herself for engaging in her cycles of pregnancies and abortions, yet she felt compelled to repeat this behavior and had little understanding of what was driving her treacherous activity. Annie was blindly starving herself to death and Dawn's panic attacks seemed to her like "bolts out of the blue" and she had no way of understanding them.

As these patients gained greater awareness and understanding of their inner worlds and of the fantasies and forces that were causing their disquiet, their symptoms and dysfunctional behaviors were greatly reduced. It is important to emphasize, however, that this increased insight did not come about through an intellectual discussion, but rather through an emotion-laden exploration of internal conflicts, remembering forgotten painful memories and by the in vivo experiencing and interpretation of the internal struggles that were resurrected and enacted with the therapist in the transference situation.

Whereas in the early decades of practicing insight-oriented psychotherapy, the primary therapeutic effort was to increase self-awareness, to uncover buried memories, and unearth the dynamic forces and conflicts of the mind, in more recent years the treatment relationship itself has been more rigorously examined and has been appreciated as an important element in the therapeutic process. Aspects of the intense relationship that have been considered to serve a therapeutic function include, offering a model for identification and growth, the experiencing of a new kind of interpersonal connection, affording an important source for self-esteem building, engaging in an interpersonal "dance" that illuminates the nuances of an individual's habitual interactions, being a source of human nurturance and reality testing, and to provide a model for self-reflection and self-analytic functioning. The matrix of the intense therapeutic relationship offers opportunities for such experience and growth.

These two aspects of the therapeutic process—developing greater insight and engaging in a new and growth-stimulating relationship—are tightly bound together in the treatment situation. The particular mix of these elements, however, varies with each individual patient's psychological needs. Indeed, "one size does not fit all." With Claude and Diana efforts to build on the relationship in establishing a higher level of reality testing and to enhance self-esteem were paramount. Whereas for Joan and Dawn, greater emphasis was placed in clarifying the unconscious dynamics and fantasies that motivated their symptomatic and dysfunctional behaviors.

In our work to understand and treat emotional distress, we open paths to better appreciate the conflicts and forces that are integral to the human condition. In a parallel way, by examining the subtleties and complexities of the two-person therapeutic encounter, we are afforded a window for exploring the nuances of human relatedness. The multiple levels and modes of interpersonal communication, utilizing words, gestures, affective attunement, empathic immersion, unconscious cues, and mirroring, and intersubjective experience become realities in the treatment situation. In this process we more clearly acknowledge factors that serve as barriers or resistances to "hearing" another person's fears and internal struggles as well as coming to better value those qualities of interpersonal relationships that lend themselves to synergy and creativity.

Insight-oriented, psychoanalytically informed psychotherapy is often seen in the public forum as a mysterious treatment intervention to be discussed only in whispers. Whereas new robotic surgical procedures and the myriad of pills and medications advanced to do miraculous things to body and soul are loudly promoted in the media, discussions about psychotherapy or consulting with a therapist are often kept secret. Several years ago a respected leader of a national mental health group counseled college applicants, that if asked, they should not reveal in their health records if they had ever seen a psychiatrist. To so indicate, he advised, would only lead to administrative complications that they would come to regret.

The ongoing collusion in our society to keep in the shadows consulting with a mental health professional and the process of psychotherapy create a certain aura of mystification. In such a secretive and insulated climate, misunderstanding and distortions can easily flourish. Public media and the popular entertainment world regularly add to such misrepresentations. For instance, in the entertainment world, psychotherapists have traditionally been seen as "strange" people and objects for lampooning. This was epitomized in such movies as, *Shrink* (2009), *The President's Analyst* (1967), *Lovesick* (1983), *Analyze This* (1999), and many more. In recent years Doctor Jennifer Melfi in the popular TV series *The Sopranos* was depicted more kindly, though from published reviews, it was the therapist's shapely legs rather than her technical skills that drew most of the attention.

Starting in 2008 a cable TV series entitled *In Treatment* wherein the work of a dynamic psychotherapist and his several patients are depicted with considerable candor and sensitivity.

The production enjoyed remarkable success and rave reviews. The *Boston Globe* reported that the series of forty-five episodes ". . . made therapy fashionable" and "[The] script takes us to vivid distant places—all without leaving the therapist's office." The popularity of this show was related to the dramatic depiction of a variety of life's struggles and tragedies—narratives that were real and easily identifiable by the empathic viewer. Included in these narratives was a young adult battling with cancer and denying her dependency needs, a suicidal executive haunted by ghosts from his past], and an unfulfilled lawyer desperately trying to remedy old wounds. In addition to these gripping stories, the TV audience was also afforded an intimate view of what went on in "talking treatments." The dialogues between patient and therapist, their emotional involvement, and struggles were dramatically depicted. The authenticity of these encounters, the impact on the viewer drawn into the treatment relationship, and breaching the usual boundaries of such therapeutic encounters were elements that made the TV drama compelling.

In 1954 Dr. Robert Lindner, a psychoanalyst, wrote a now-classic book entitled *The Fifty-Minute Hour: A Collection of True Psychoanalytic Tales.* In considerable detail the author described five patients he treated in psychoanalytically informed therapy. He outlined his patient's presenting difficulties, their past histories, his understanding of their dysfunction, and the treatment process. Lindner's effort to shed light on the drama in his consulting room, and the unfolding progression between his patients and himself, were considered heroic and somewhat heretical in the 1950s. He revealed the intimacies of the treatment relationship—a relationship that was generally shrouded in mystery. Lindner's book gained great popularity and became an important contribution to the literature.

Though written over a half-century ago, some of Lindner's

observations about psychoanalytically informed treatment remain insightful and prophetic.

"Around psychoanalysis there has been built a fence of mystery and something resembling awe . . . This cabalistic climate which today surrounds the practice of psychoanalysis has had some weird and, I think, harmful effects. Not the least among them has been the conversion of the psychoanalyst—in the public mind, at least—to a kind of devil's disciple who works with means arcane and mystic to secure the transformations of character or personality he desires.

"Nothing could be further from the truth. Neither the science of psychoanalysis nor the art of its practice depend upon extraordinary agencies. As a matter of fact, the only medium employed by the analyst is the commonest instrument of all— his own human self, utilized to the fullest in an effort to understand its fellows.

"The gradual replacement of men by machines to execute the functions of life is a characteristic of our time . . . But there is one area where no machine, no matter how complex, no matter how inspired, can act for its maker. This is the area of understanding, of sympathetic comprehension, of intimate, knowing communication between one being and the next. Now and forever, only man will fathom men."

Lindner goes on,

". . . it is [the psychoanalyst's] sensitivity—in short, the analyst's own person—which is the single instrument, the only tool, with which he performs. Only on himself, and on nothing else, does he depend . . . That this agent [the analyst] is only a mere human, just another person with his own hopes and fears, goals and anxieties, prejudices and pretensions, weaknesses and strengths, is really the heart of the matter . . ."

Transference, a ubiquitous element in all human associations, was described in my Introduction to *Nine Lives* in the following way: "Individuals bring to all human relationships their past experience, their conscious and unconscious wishes, expectations and fantasies. These internal dynamic factors color and mold how one experiences the important people and events around them. This includes how the patient experiences the therapist."

Just as the patient brings his history and inner experience to the consultation room, the therapist carries into the therapeutic relationship his unique and dynamic inner world and his conscious and unconscious experience of his patient. This transference of the therapist to the particular patient is called "countertransference." The therapist's awareness of his countertransference to this person, and the feelings and fantasies that are stirred up within him by the patient are of considerable importance for two primary reasons: (1) such countertransference responses in the therapist may produce certain "blind spots," or areas of acute sensitivity which might confuse and derail the treatment process. For instance, a particularly dependent patient might anger a therapist who has his own inner conflicts about dependency needs, and the therapist might find himself irritated, overindulgent, or deaf to his patient's inner struggle. Hopefully the mental health professional, because of his own personal therapy and sensitivity, is able to appreciate and understand his vulnerabilities and such "blind spots" are minimized. (2) The therapist's awareness of his emotional responses and his fantasies related to this particular individual may be an extremely important avenue to his patient's inner world better, his past experiences, and how his patient relates to his surroundings.

The psychotherapist's countertransference or more generally his feelings and responses to his patient are his stethoscope—an essential way of listening to his patient's heart and inner world.

For instance, after many months of treating Claude and there being little apparent change, I began to feel hopeless, helpless, and ready to give up. Though in the early months of the hospitalization I felt angry at his parents for simply "depositing" their son in our facility, as I began to taste my own despair and urge to abandon Claude, I came to appreciate how his parents had given up on Claude. They were feeling hopeless, and they just wanted to return home to their other children and forget their ill son. Claude, in turn was adept at getting the people around him—his parents and his therapist—to abandon him and in so doing complete his self-protective and selfdestructive isolation.

At times Annie made me feel like an emotional "yo-yo." Sobbing and with great anguish she screamed, "Help me, help me I desperately need your help—but get away don't talk to me—if you help me I will feel more helpless and worse about myself." This pull–push that characterized our early treatment relationship was confusing, unsettling, and disquieting—but once I understood the meaning of this "dance," I began to have a clearer picture of the unconscious struggle going on inside Annie's world—an internal struggle which was driving her to distraction and self-destruction.

There were times when I felt the urge to be the supportive father Henry so craved and to give him advice as to how he might improve his life. I knew, however, that such direction would not be helpful. Many people at work and in his community gave him such advice but this was of minimal benefit—and yet he stirred up in me this urge to so intervene. I came to see that my paternalistic inclinations in large part were in response to Henry's "father hunger" and to his sense of inner emptiness. It was important for Henry to come to understand and come to terms with his tragic childhood loss and for us not try to "gloss over" or trivialize his struggle with his anger and his sense of alienation. To instruct him on leading a better life would have left him feeling misunderstood and further estranged.

In my focus on the nine lives described in this book, and in the process of trying to better appreciate aspects of emotional dysfunction and the therapeutic process, there remain many ambiguities, complexities, and unanswered questions. Though initially such open-ended queries seem daunting, such questions will lead to better and more refined questions and hopefully lead to an expansion of our understanding of the human condition.

APPENDIX—ADDITIONAL NOTES AND ANALYTIC MATERIAL

have described in the nine clinical vignettes, some of the ongoing work of intensive, psychoanalytically informed psychotherapy. To further clarify and demystify aspects of this process, I present below more detailed material from the therapy sessions. I include (1) My rough process notes describing the dialogue and analytic unfolding from a single session in Annie's treatment, and (2) A focused longitudinal study of Frankie's changing coping skills over several years in treatment.

To establish a context for the actual clinical pictures, I refer the reader back to earlier chapters in this book—to the narratives of Annie and Frankie.

1. The details of a single hour with Annie:

This session takes place after nearly two years of intensive therapy— meeting five times each week. At this point Annie remains emaciated and continues to look physically ill. She has graduated with honors from her high school; she is attending a local university and living in the dormitory. Annie had elected to attend the local university so that she could continue her treatment. The following session occurs early on a Monday morning—one month into her first college semester. My practice was to spend ten to fifteen minutes after every session writing my notes about the session. The notations below with almost verbatim dialogue are minimally edited from the original handwritten records.

[Annie was sitting in my waiting room when I came out of my office. She wore a thick formless sweater hiding her body. Her face remains emaciated and pale and her hair looked more disheveled than usual. She appeared sullen, depressed, and agitated.]

ANNIE:—[*Silence*] . . . I have got to do something . . . I can't go on like this . . . got to get a hold of the situation . . . it's impossible. I'm just too weak, a wimp, a follower . . . I just go along with things . . . no strength, no conviction or ideas of what I have to do. I just react and go along with things. (*All this is said in a tearful somewhat agitated tone.*).

[*She gives many details of a variety of weekend events—she had been up until six a.m. the previous day—socializing— "goofing around"—her dorm room has become a hub of social activity with friends, telling each other stories from high school—all this is related with a sense of pleasure and smiling.*]
. . . But then I' m not getting my schoolwork done. It's piling up . . . impossible . . . terrible [again tearful and agitated] . . .

THERAPIST:—Sounds like a difficult situation when you feel yourself caught in the middle—there is the struggle inside you that if you let yourself enjoy goofing around, your friends, socializing—then you feel pulled in the other direction—like you are not allowed to mess around and somehow lose control, let things just happen—which we know always worries you a lot . . .

ANNIE:—[*increasingly upset, sitting with her head down*] I was talking with my father last night—telling him that I really wasn't doing my work, my classes are boring, wasting my time at college—maybe I shouldn't be at college—no goals, I have no idea why I'm there, floundering, etc. . . . And the worst thing [*actively crying and sobbing*] I'm fat!! So self-conscious . . . I don't know what to do . . . every thing is falling apart. . . I'm falling apart [*increasingly agitated. hits the chair, and punches her leg, shouting.*] . . . I need some advice!! . . . suggestions of what to do . . . I just can't do it . . . I don't know how to go on.

THERAPIST:—What do you mean?

ANNIE:—How do I stop eating? And then the work problem—I'm falling behind. And it's not that I feel fat—I am fat!! [*screaming with tears rolling down her face*]

THERAPIST:—Annie, what kind of help do you think would be helpful?

ANNIE:—Advice, direction, suggestions! How can I stop eating? What should I do about college? I can't go on; tell me what to do!

THERAPIST:—Well Annie I hear you—but we've seen over and over again how that kind of help—advice, suggestions, directions make you feel bad about yourself—more helpless, more unable to cope with the feelings inside yourself and how you feel about yourself, how angry . . .

ANNIE:—(*interrupts* Therapist's *["NF OK? Or identify?] sentence and shouts*) BULLSHIT!! I don't believe it! You must have some ideas how I can manage—what I should do. If you'd tell me your ideas—your advice—I would have something to go on, some direction, some path I should follow . . . (*shouting, crying, banging her fists on the chair . . . a full-blown temper tantrum*)

THERAPIST:—(*said with some firmness*) Hold on a minute Annie—let's step back a minute and look at what's going on between the two of us. We started today's session with how upset you were with yourself because you felt you were just going along with all kinds of outside pressures—at the dorm with friends, with your dad and his advice . . . You felt helpless, no input from you, no self-direction, compliant when you go along with what people's pressure and advice . . . yet now you're demanding that I tell you what to do, how to manage, give you advice, direction . . . so you can respond to me by complying or more likely rejecting what I say. We've seen this pattern over and over again here and at home. It's clear that it upsets you, you get very angry when you feel you are being pushed, directed, guided—yet at the same time demand, invite that I tell you what to do, give you an agenda— that I somehow take control over you. It's the pull–push thing we've seen over and over in here and outside here. You demand I take over—'but if you do I will feel worse and worse, more and more helpless and bad about myself.'

ANNIE:—(*long silence . . . Annie seems much calmer and in control. Takes tissues from my Kleenex box—blows her nose and wipes her eyes. Seems reflective and calmly goes on.*) I don't know what I'll do . . . Maybe I'll keep that appointment with my academic advisor . . . (smiles . . .) Maybe the best thing would be to go back to my room and take a nap—exhausted—I didn't get much sleep over the weekend. See you tomorrow *(session ends).*

During the ten minutes after this session while I made my notes—I felt a somewhat uneasy and dissatisfied. Though I thought my intervention was accurate and timely, I wondered if Annie's temper tantrum and my firmer than usual comments represented some form of enactment—Annie seemed out of control, and I intruded and verbally provided restraint. Were we reenacting her 'push–pull' struggle, and were the words I said less important than the interplay between us? . . . I was left uncertain and questioning . . .

2. A longitudinal view over three years—Frankie

In this view of the analytic process, I will focus on one specific psychological struggle of the patient and how this changed during the three-year period in his therapy. The seven-year-old child Frankie was described in an earlier chapter. In addition to Frankie's unhappiness and his propensity to getting himself beaten up at school, Frankie struggled for many years with separations. Such periods of separation were fraught with considerable anxiety and regressive behavior. Historically there were several relevant events related to his separation anxiety. When Frankie was born, mother felt the need to return to her full-time professional work two weeks after Frankie was born, and his father initially seemed uninterested in his new role. A fulltime caretaker was employed. Even when both parents were home, they retreated to their respective offices and relegated Frankie's care to babysitters. When Frankie was two years old, his mother had to enter a hospital for a ten-day period. The parent did nothing to prepare Frankie for this separation believing that since Frankie did not yet talk, the separation would not have meaning or impact for the infant.

Mid-June and early September were always difficulty times for

Frankie. At these times he was increasingly anxious and "clingy." The family practice was that both parents worked full-time. Every year in June, the live-in caregiver was discharged and the family divided up and left for separate working vacations abroad. Frankie remained with his mother, though a new caregiver was hired to take care of Frankie while his mother pursued her research activities in Europe. The father went off on his own to another part of the Continent to do his work. In the fall, the family reunited at home, a new caregiver was employed, and the parents continued their full-time work. There were five such caregivers in the child's first five years. Frankie was always quite tearful and upset during each of these disruptions.

During the three-and-one-half year period of analysis (four sessions / week) there were three two-month-long summer interruptions of the therapeutic work when parents felt it was necessary to return to Europe with Frankie.

As might be predicted from the historical material, the periods prior to our treatment separations would be difficult for this youngster. I will sketch some of the treatment hours during the one-month periods before each of these summer separations in an effort to underscore the changes in Frankie's dealing with these disruptions.

Period prior to the separation of the first year

Frankie had been in the analysis for nine months prior to the first summer vacation and was well engaged in the analytic work. He was verbal, curious, thoughtful, and vivacious in sessions. His fantasy life, as reflected in his play, was rich and affectladen. Several times he started a session by telling me about a boy he knew in school who really needed to see a psychiatrist.

As we approached the summer, Frankie became increasingly quiet and subdued. He appeared to withdraw and become detached. Frankie then brought in a Monopoly game from home, and in the last four weeks prior to the separation he pressed to play Monopoly during *every* session. This behavior was atypical for Frankie; previously his play and activity in the consultation room had been quite varied. The Monopoly games were continuous, seemed to occupy all of his attention, and were driven by a great deal of pressure. He appeared engrossed, and his remarks were almost totally involved with the Monopoly play. If a game ended in the middle of a session, Frankie began setting up the board for a second game. A game that was not completed by the end of an hour was carried over and continued without pause to the next appointment. He reported planning his strategy in the waiting room before the sessions began. He cautioned me to be "conservative" in my moves and to be sure not to "overextend" myself.

My multiple and varied efforts to explore, clarify, and interpret this *monopolizing* activity were met with a verbal or behavioral expression of "just play, don't talk." My many comments about the defensive function of this preoccupation and the affects that seemed to surround the impending separation appeared to further the entrenchment and emotional withdrawal. On occasion, when I was in the midst of a comment, Frankie would not wait and would move my token around the board himself—a gesture that further negated my presence in the office.

In the very last session before the summer interruption, Frankie played Monopoly with increased gusto and began setting up the board for a new game in the last ten minutes of the hour. He appeared to ignore my comments. Having previously mentioned the fall schedule and the date of the first session after the vacation, I gave Frankie an appointment card for September. Frankie slipped the card into the Monopoly board and said he planned to take this game on vacation with him.

The period prior to the separation of the second year

As the second year of the analysis began, Frankie readily shared with me many anecdotes about his summer vacation. He drew numerous diagrams of the places he had visited and spoke of many exciting, stimulating, and at times worrisome events including fights with his cousins. The analytic material during the second year was rich, and the analytic work progressed well. As we approached the summer separation, the affective quality and the content of the analytic material began to shift. Frankie again became more withdrawn and increasingly preoccupied. At times we would lapse into periods of staring at my face. When this was noted, Frankie would say that he was "just thinking," but he was not sure what was on his mind.

In this four-week period Frankie brought in, or devised a large number of games. Some of these games, such as tossing checkers into a box, were quite solitary and excluded me. Most of the games he brought from home, and games he insisted that his father buy for him, were war games. A game called Battle Cry was his favorite. He also constructed a new game called "Attack" using soldiers and blocks. Frankie was very involved in these war games, and during this period there were many sessions when he had difficulty stopping at the end of the hour. There would then be a last-minute frantic effort to clean up the playroom. In one session he aggressively started snipping at loose threads on my upholstered chair with a scissors. He brought in his Monopoly game two or three times during this month, but it held little interest for him.

During this one-month period, Frankie was actively preparing for his vacation. He made countless lists of things he had to buy or things he had to prepare to bring with him. He often commented as he struggled with a new detailed list, "I keep thinking

I've forgotten something." For the first time he spoke of his worries about the trip, of accidents and robbers, and was quite interested in telling me the story of Robinson Crusoe. He became worried one day when he could not locate a lost checker in my office. Frankie asked the specific date the sessions would resume, and he noted from the appointment card how strangely I spelled my last name. He showed increased curiosity about the consultation room, the heater, the file, and then wondered how much money I made each year. He made a thick book of index cards, a "memory book," in which to write down the things he wanted to remember. Once when he ran out of cards, he repeatedly reminded me to be sure to buy some more. The next day as I went to meet him in the waiting room, he immediately blurted out, "Did you remember to get the cards?" In the last session before the summer vacation, Frankie straightened out a desk drawer that he had come to identify as his. He made a sign indicating that this drawer belonged to him. He threw away some old pictures and paper scraps that he said were no longer of interest to him, and he put the crayons and pencils in order. He then tried to construct a secret code with letters, numbers, and symbols, but it was so complicated that he became frustrated and threw away the "master copy."

The period prior to the separation of the third year

In the early part of the month prior to this third summer vacation, Frankie went on a several-day class outing. This was his first such trip away from his parents, and he was quite excited. He counted the days to the excursion, and during one of our appointments he prepared a long list of clothing, books, and games he would need to pack. He was especially hopeful that he would be able to stay in the same cabin with his male teacher. At the same time, he now decided to move his room at home, up to the third floor. His parents had coaxed him to do this for several years, but he had resisted the change, saying that he was afraid to be alone. His new room was larger, and he would now not have to share his parents' bathroom. With great pride he drew the floor plan of his new room for me and indicated where he had placed all the furniture. During this one-month period he became very interested in citizens band radios and borrowed a library book on how to build his own walkie-talkie. He wondered how the transatlantic cable worked, and with considerable affect talked of how he would miss his friends during the vacation period.

Frankie became very involved first in drawing and then in constructing in three dimensions many spacecraft and space stations. The space stations were to be places where astronauts could stop for rest and relaxation in their celestial travels. The craft were very elaborate, had all sorts of living facilities, and carried large crystals for energy storage. The dimensions of the craft were scaled according to multiples of my office; for example, three times the size of the playroom, twice as wide as the couch. On a few occasions Frankie noted that they had a psychiatrist on the spaceship, because the astronauts might need someone with whom to talk. Some unknown enemy frequently shot at the spacecraft. When I tried to clarify some of the wishes, conflicts, and fears reflected in this fantasy play, Frankie told me an idea he had of taking me and my office in a large rocket on the voyage with him, but only if I did not ask any questions.

On several occasions during his pre-vacation period, Frankie commented on how comfortable the easy chair was in my office and how it fit his back "just perfectly." Frankie asked to play checkers so he could learn some of my tricks, and maybe this year he could finally beat his uncle in Europe.

In a session two weeks prior to the vacation, Frankie was talking about the excitement and the dangers of space travel. After I commented on the excitement but also some of the worries about the upcoming separation, Frankie became very quiet and reflective. He then asked about a picture and a plant that had been removed from my office during the previous summer vacation. He recalled vividly where everything had been laid out in the office twelve months earlier.

During the last two weeks Frankie asked several times to play cards. The card games he chose were solitaire and Liar. Solitaire was a game his mother had taught him to play when he was bored or lonesome. The Liar game, which involved faking and deceiving the opponent, led to concerns and questions of whether I was trustworthy, and would I be there when he returned. During on such games Frankie inquired as to the exact date when the sessions would resume. The associations surrounding this material brought up for the first time early memories of the several caregivers who disappeared each summer and who were then replaced in the fall. Frankie vividly recalled how one woman smoked so much that it made him cough all the time. He noted that he still did not like it when people smoked around him.

In the last week before the summer separation, Frankie became involved in drawing his ideal vacation island, a place where everything would be pleasant and relaxing. This large drawing took almost three sessions to complete. Initially, he worked on the rugged outline of an irregular landmass that was in the middle of the ocean. It was to be just for him, a place where he could relax. Frankie then made several secret and well-protected ports for boats. The drawings became more and more complex with several streams, lakes, roads, and then houses. He then allowed that maybe he would have several of his good friends live on the island since that would be more fun. The interior of the island became more complex with storehouses, amusement areas, and "nice shady areas for fishing." Frankie then drew several adjoining islands with interconnecting bridges and said that maybe it would be OK if I lived on one of these islands.

Discussion

In comparing the one-month periods prior to the three summer separations, it becomes clear that Frankie's response to the disruptions becomes increasingly more complex and adaptive. A progressively broader and more reality-based array of coping techniques were mobilized in response to the impending loss. In the first one-month period, Frankie struggled, in a pressured and almost desperate manner, to exclude and deny the upcoming separation. His monopolizing play was in part an attempt to avoid thinking and feeling about the impending loss. Frankie's efforts were very much in keeping with patterns of coping with stress he had learned in his family. When he was upset at school or at home, he was encouraged to keep busy with his lessons, was given a new toy, or was taught to play solitaire.

In the second, and even more in the third pre-separation periods, Frankie was clearly and more directly dealing with the imminent loss. The manifest themes of our work related to preparation for trips, memory books, space travel, lonesome astronauts, being lost and forgotten, danger of voyages, long-distance communications, questions about continuity and trust, feelings of sadness, and missing friends. These issues and the underlying conflicts were repeatedly talked about, elaborated on, clarified and interpreted. Talking about his imaginations and fears related to loss and abandonment was evident throughout our work together, but in the preseparation periods, these issues moved into the foreground of the therapeutic arena. In this process, Frankie developed considerable understanding at a level appropriate for a latency-age child. It became evident that he had grown and was better able to deal with separation and in the ability to establish "bridges" between himself and others.

www.ingramcontent.com/pod-product-compliance
Lightning Source LLC
Chambersburg PA
CBHW060237030426
42335CB00014B/1497